AF378200

• HALSGROVE DISCOVER SERIES ➤

SNOWDONIA

WALKS FROM THE CARNEDDAU TO CADAIR IDRIS

Jerry Rawson

HALSGROVE

First published in Great Britain in 2005

Copyright © 2005 text and photographs, Jerry Rawson

Frontispiece photograph: *Tryfan and the Ogwen Valley.*

Disclaimer
While the author has walked all the routes described in the book, no responsibility can be
accepted for any omissions or errors or for any future changes that may occur in the details given.
The author and publisher cannot accept any liability for accident, mishap or loss arising from the use of this book.

*All rights reserved. No part of this publication may be reproduced,
stored in a retrieval system, or transmitted in any form or by any means
without the prior permission of the copyright holder.*

British Library Cataloguing-in-Publication Data
A CIP record for this title is available from the British Library

ISBN 1 84114 429 0

HALSGROVE
Halsgrove House
Lower Moor Way
Tiverton, Devon EX16 6SS
Tel: 01884 243242
Fax: 01884 243325
email: sales@halsgrove.com
website: www.halsgrove.com

Printed and bound by D'Auria Industrie Grafiche Spa, Italy

CONTENTS

AUTHOR'S ACKNOWLEDGEMENTS

I would like to acknowledge the help and support from my wife Katy Rawson with proof reading, artwork and maps and also Roly Smith, editorial manager for Halsgrove and president of the Outdoor Writers' Guild, for his guidance and editorial help. I would also like to thank all the friends and strangers alike who patiently posed for photographs.

WALK LOCATIONS

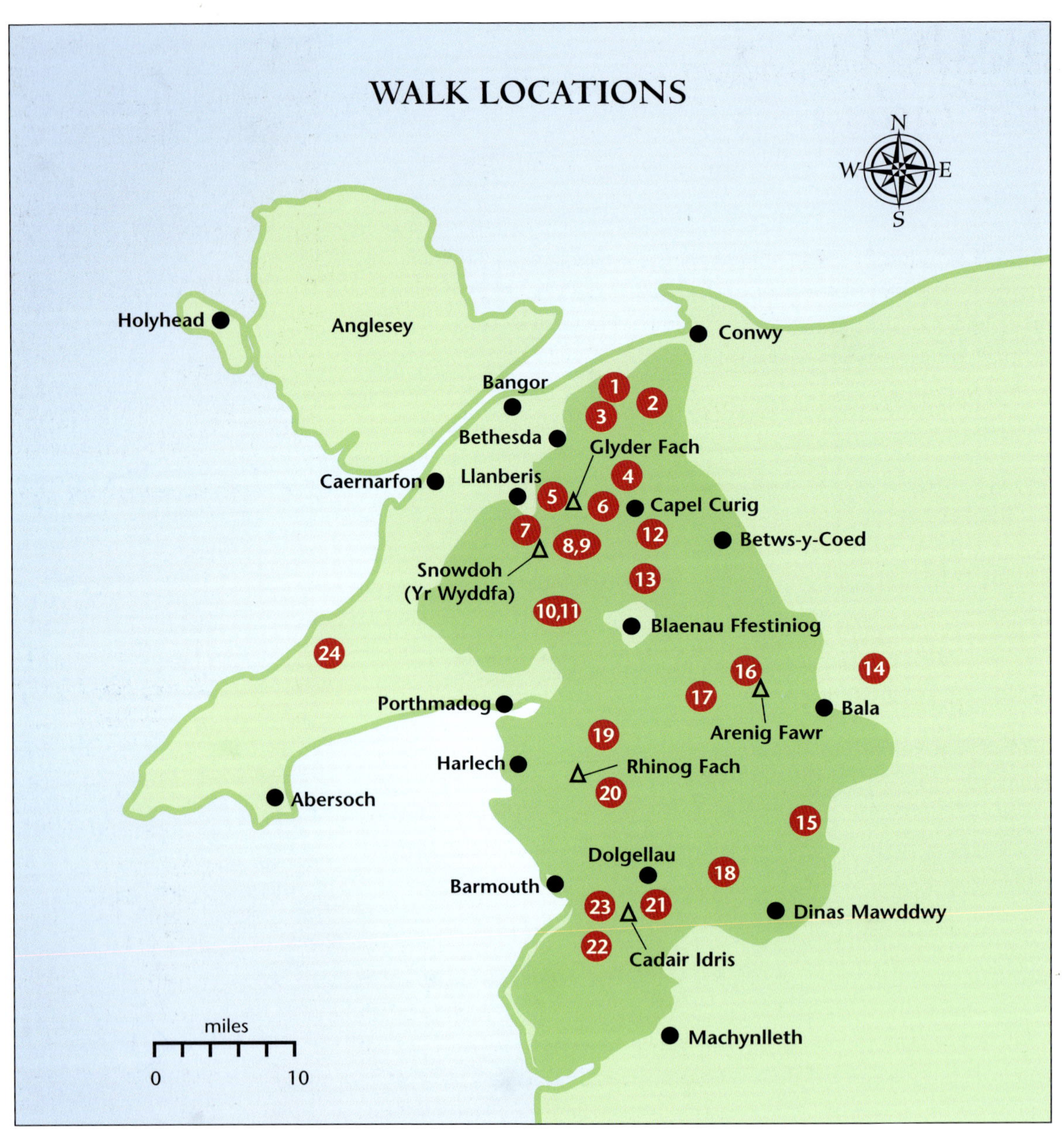

INTRODUCTION
The place of eagles

For those who enjoy ascending soaring rocky ridges to isolated mountain summits; seeking out dramatic ice-carved cwms and hidden lakes; crossing huge whaleback ridges and open moorland; exploring magnificent coastal scenery, or simply following gentle river courses through beautiful wooded valleys, then Snowdonia has it all – and much more. This book explores these wild hills, seeking out the hidden corners which make Snowdonia such a very special place.

The Snowdonia National Park – Parc Cenedlaethol Eryri in Welsh – was designated as a National Park in 1951 and lies in the north-west corner of Wales. Eryri, the Welsh name for Snowdonia, is translated from 'eryr' meaning eagle, hence 'land or place of eagles', although it is now thought that the name may come from a medieval Welsh word meaning a 'high place'. Then Eryri would mean 'land of mountains', which is very apt since it contains some of the most spectacular, and tightly packed, mountain scenery south of Scotland.

Snowdonia is a land of heather moors, lakes, wooded valleys and craggy, mountain ranges. Within the boundary of the 2,142 sq km (827 square mile) National Park there are 37km (23 miles) of coastline with beaches, sand dunes, and great sweeping bays such as Tremadog and Mawddach. This means that from many mountain summits you catch glimpses of the sea.

Snowdonia consists of four main different types of rocks – Pre-Cambrian, Cambrian, Ordovician and Silurian – which, combined with the forces of submersion, earth movement, lifting and erosion, have created the many facets of the landscape. Even the youngest rock, the Silurian, is over 400 million years old. But the final shaping of the landscape we see today was brought about relatively recently during the Ice Ages. Glaciers only disappeared about 10,000 years ago leaving behind U-shaped valleys,

Foel Goch seen across Llyn Ogwen.

The stream flowing from Llyn Idwal, with Y Garn in the background.

Looking north from Moel Hebog.

cwms, glacial lakes, moraines and numerous erratic boulders. Cwm Idwal is a classic place where many of these features can be seen.

Humans have also influenced the landscape stretching back over 6,000 years ever since Neolithic people started to settle and farm here, through the Bronze and Iron Ages, the Roman occupation, and the Middle Ages, up to the present. Sheep farming, mining for minerals and slate quarrying have all left their mark on the landscape during the last few centuries. Quarrying still exists, albeit on a smaller scale than previously, and although many of the relics from mining and quarrying still remain, nature is steadily reclaiming the ruins, which are still a fascinating feature in many parts of Snowdonia.

A standing stone on the western flanks of Cadair Idris.

Right: *Crossing the ridge linking Moelwyn Bach to Moelwyn Mawr.*

Above: *Tryfan seen from the outflow of Llyn Ogwen.*

Top left: *Snowdon (Yr Wyddfa) in its winter cloak.*

Left: *Tryfan and Glyder Fach.*

Ascending Crib y Ddysgl, with Crib Goch in the background.

Crossing Snowdon's northern peaks. Moel Eilio in the distance.

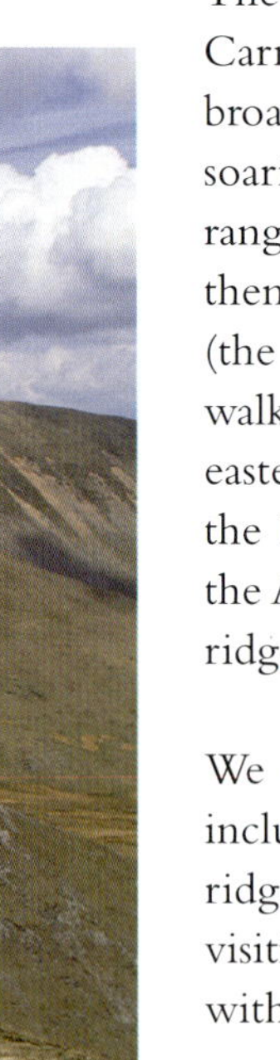

The walks

The selected walks in this book explore the main mountain groups and cover the various types of scenery in Snowdonia. But they also reflect its many and varied facets such as geology, people, history and the working landscape. Most of the walks are situated within the National Park, and by grouping them into nine reasonably well-defined geographical areas, it means that a trip to any one will give a choice of several walks.

The walks range from relatively easy ones up small hills, to some demanding expeditions over wild mountain terrain, where high fitness levels and map and compass skills are essential, especially in bad weather. In winter conditions, some of the featureless and more inhospitable parts of Snowdonia can be very unforgiving for the ill-prepared walker, and the terrain demands respect at all times.

The walks start from the vast rolling plateaux of the Carneddau, where you can stride out for miles below broad skies, then the neighbouring rocky cwms and soaring ridges of Tryfan and the Glyder (Y Glyderau) range are explored. The craggy ramparts of Snowdon then beckon, before the grassy hills of the Nantlle range (the Eifionydd) are visited. In marked contrast, we then walk the shapely Moelwyn (Y Moelwyninion) hills. The eastern edges of Snowdonia also provide great walks on the Berwyn (Y Berwynion), the Arenig (Y Arenig) and the Aran (Yr Aran), which lie along the broad, undulating ridge between Llangollen and Machynlleth.

We then move out west to explore the coastal regions including Yr Eifl on the Lleyn Peninsula, the rugged ridges of the Rhinog (Y Rhinogau) mountains, finally visiting the impressive southern sentinel of Cadair Idris, with its broad ridges and hanging cwms.

A few of the described walks, such as Tryfan's North Ridge and the Snowdon Horseshoe, also involve some scrambling and are potentially more serious. Scrambling is that grey, adventurous area where hill-walking and rock-climbing meet. It means that uphill progress involves using your hands as well as your feet, often in dramatic situations, where skills and judgment are pre-requisites to a safe passage. Often some of the best ways up Snowdonia's mountains are scrambles along narrow ridges and up steep arêtes; for example Bristly Ridge up to the summit of Glyder Fach.

Scrambles are usually graded on a scale of 1 to 3. Grade 1 scrambles are relatively straightforward, like the Crib Goch pinnacles on Snowdon, whereas Grade 2 usually means that you need more technical skills and the terrain is often steeper. Grade 3 scrambles are much more serious, steeper and technical, and involve basic skills in rock climbing plus an ability to use a rope when the terrain demands it. All scrambling is potentially dangerous, since it is usually done without a rope. As you gain experience you will find that scrambling in Snowdonia can provide magnificent days out which last long in the memory. If you wish to learn more then it is worth going out with someone experienced or taking a course on basic rope skills at a reputable centre.

Ascending Y Gribin, with Tryfan in the background.

Scrambling up Bristly Ridge.

Pleasant scrambling up the East Ridge of Y Garn.

Approaching Cnicht from Croesor.

The impressive ice-carved Cwm Cau, Cadair Idris.

The described routes are all on public rights of way, access land or open country and with the recent implementation of the Countryside and Rights of Way (CROW) Act 2000 in Wales, access to areas once forbidden has now improved. Many of the walks are circular, and mainly covered by the appropriate 1:25,000 Ordnance Survey or Harvey Superwalker maps. The text is merely intended to whet the appetite for a particular area and to encourage the reader to sit down with a map and work out the routes.

The times given for the routes are only a general guideline and assume the walk will be undertaken in reasonable weather conditions. Based on terrain, height ascended and total distance covered, I have indicated the relative seriousness of a walk by grading it easy, moderate, difficult or very difficult. I hope this personal choice of walks will encourage readers to go and discover the areas for themselves, and I apologise if your favourite walking area has been left out.

Most of the starting points for the walks have reasonable parking and many are also accessible by public transport including good rail access along with a network of bus routes. For details use the National Traveline Tel: 0870 608 2608 or www.traveline.org.uk. For details of the Snowdon Sherpa bus service see the National Park web site at www.eryri-npa.co.uk. The main bus and train operator in North Wales is Arriva; see www.arriva.co.uk or www.arrivatrainswales.co.uk.

A wide range of hotels, B&Bs and camping and caravan site accommodation is available; for more details see www.stayinwales.co.uk, www.campingandcaravanclub.co.uk. For information about youth hostel accommodation see www.yha.org. Tourist information is available on www.visitwales.com and also at various National Park Information Centres and also the Snowdonia National Park Authority site at www.eryri-npa.co.uk.

Maps and Place Names

Welsh names of places and mountains are very descriptive, as the language has changed little over the centuries. For example, Betws-y-Coed means 'prayer house (Betws) in the woods (Coed)' and the mountain Carnedd Llewelyn, means 'the cairn (Carnedd) of Llewelyn.' The words for landscape features include 'afon' for a river, 'bwlch' for a pass and 'llyn' for a lake.

However, there is often difficulty regarding the correct spellings of some Welsh names of places and mountain ranges. You even find variations between different maps. Because of this I have used mainly spellings from the latest available OS maps at the time of writing, which is consistent with recent guidebooks to walking and rock climbing in Snowdonia. This approach may not please all Welsh linguists so I apologise in advance for any errors or inconsistencies that might appear in the text.

If you want to find out more about the Welsh language and place names, then I recommend *Enwau Eryri – Place-names in Snowdonia,* by Iwan Arfon Jones and also an excellent web site developed by the Ordnance Survey in 2004 about the Welsh language and place names of Wales: www.ordnancesurvey.co.uk

Top right: *Descending the south ridge of Tryfan, with the Nant Ffrancon in the distance.*

Right: *Heading down the north-west slopes of Glyder Fawr towards Y Garn.*

Cwm Eigiau.

Crossing the rocky summit of Craig yr Isfa.

1 THE CARNEDDAU

This is a vast, comparatively featureless, rolling landscape, enclosed by the sea to the north, Bethesda and Nant Ffrancon to the west, the Ogwen Valley to the south and the Conwy Valley to the east. Its sheer size is often underestimated for the Carneddau's high and wide plateau is the largest mountain mass in North Wales, with twenty tops over 610m/2000 feet – six of them over 914m/3000 feet, including Carnedd Llewelyn and Carnedd Dafydd, the third and fourth highest mountains in Snowdonia and named after two of Wales' most famous princes. The word Carnedd (a cairn), has long been used as the name for this entire range of mountains – the Carneddau (also known as the Carnedds).

This area offers a great challenge to the keen walker who likes to stride out over great distances below wide skies. There is more high ground above 900m/3000 feet here than Central Snowdonia – pedigree enough for most. There are also spectacular hidden cwms such as Cwm Eigiau, with its fine rock climbs on the cliffs of Craig yr Ysfa, while Carnedd Dafydd's huge, gully-ridden north face known as Ysgolion Duon (the black ladders) is a winter mecca for experienced snow and ice climbers.

A combination of ridges, broad rounded summits, grassy spurs and several craggy cwms offer numerous outings to suit all tastes, from short trips to major expeditions. All the main summits are linked by a high continuous ridge, which can be traversed by a classic route from the coast at Aber to the Ogwen Valley, providing one of finest high-level walks in Snowdonia. For many walkers though, it is the great horseshoe walks penetrating into the massif which are most appealing, including the Cwm Eigiau horseshoe from the east and the Cwm Llafar circuit from Bethesda in the west. From many of the high tops you have grand views of Anglesey and the Irish Sea, Snowdon and the Glyderau, backed by distant peaks fading to the southern horizon.

Opposite: *The shapely paek of Pen Llithrig y Wrach seen from Moel Siabod.*

Looking across from Pen yr Ole Wen to Tryfan and the Glyderau.

Descending Pen yr Helgi Du towards Craig yr Isfa.

A word of warning though: in misty conditions the lack of small-scale features on the broad ridges linking the rounded tops means that competent navigation skills are essential, while in a hard winter, arctic blizzards can sweep across this Cairngorm-like plateaux. When the hills are cloaked in snow and ice, and the daylight hours are short, the Carneddau can be very unforgiving, and demand fitness, good equipment and mountaineering skills.

While the popular southern Carneddau are rugged with steep boulder-strewn slopes, craggy cwms and rocky ridges, by contrast, the secluded northern terrain is gentle and grassy, and also full of pleasant surprises such as the sight of wild ponies which breed in Ffynnon Caseg and the lovely cascades of Aber Falls. The northern side is also linked with ancient history, particularly on the seaward slopes overlooking Conwy and the lower Conwy Valley. Here is to be found a rich diversity of archaeological features.

Historically the Conwy Valley was a natural north-south access corridor, with the tributary valley of Afon Tafolog rising west of Ty'n-y-groes up to Bwlch y Ddeufaen forming the natural east-west route to the coast. The Romans built the fort of *Canovium* (or *Caerhun*) at this route junction, and the line of their road linking it with the fort of *Segonyium* at Caernarfon can still be traced over Bwlch y Ddeufaen, between the hills of Tal y Fan and the slopes of Drum. The indigenous Celtic tribe, the Ordovices ('hammer-fighters'), which ruled the west of North Wales, were nearly wiped out during the period of the Roman conquest.

The high Roman road across the northern Carneddau followed the line of an earlier prehistoric one, its route marked by a number of standing stones, including the two at Bwlch y Ddeufaen, which have given the pass its name. Extending north-east from the pass to Tal y Fan is an area rich in Neolithic and Bronze Age remains including funerary and ritual monuments and cairns. There are also standing stones, including the Cerrig Pryfaid stone circle and the Maen-y-Bardd burial chamber along with hut circles, enclosures, field walls and terraces and the fortified Iron Age settlement of Caer Bach. On the south side of the Afon Tafolog valley is the Iron Age fort of Pen-y-Gaer, with its hut circles and field systems.

This fascinating area is certainly worth exploring and is a good wet weather alternative when the higher tops are cloaked in mist.

The rounded summits of the Eastern Carneddau.

Shapely Pen yr Ole Wen seen from Llyn Idwal.

Crossing the broad ridge linking Carnedd Llewelyn and Carnedd Dafydd.

Approaching Drosgl, with Moel Wnion in the background.

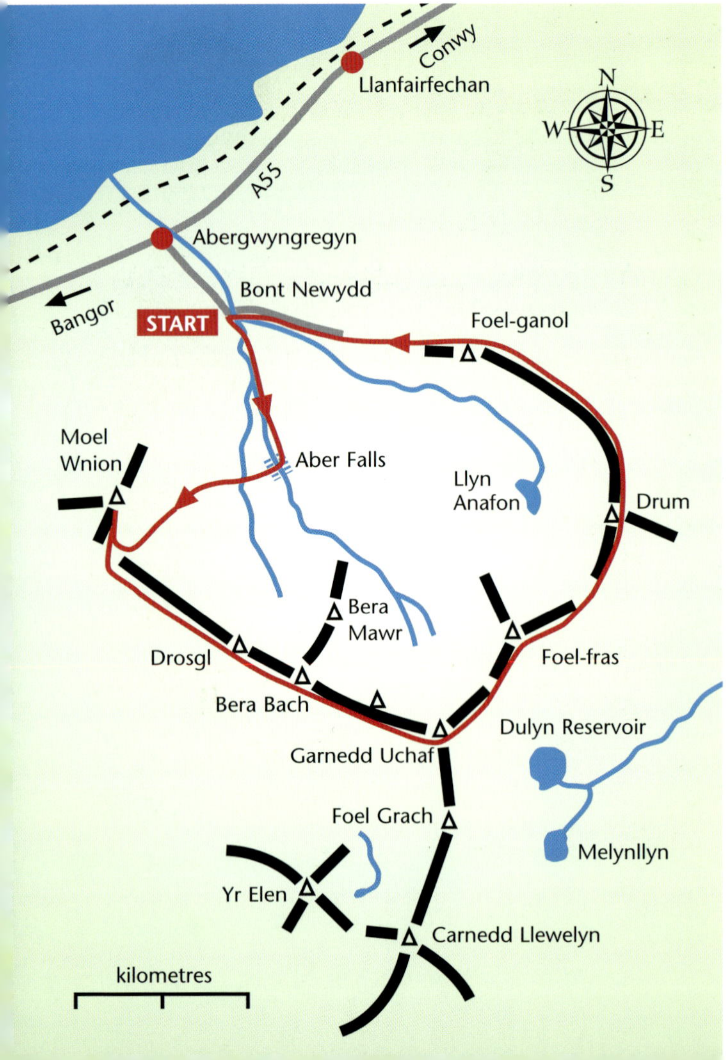

This splendid walk, mainly off the beaten track, starts from Abergwyngregyn (Aber for short), just off the A55 North Wales coast road, south-west of Llanfairfechan. The circuit is a natural horseshoe of high hills whose rivers drain into Conwy Bay to the north of the spectacular Aber Falls. Along the walk you have some excellent views over waves of hills rolling south-west towards Snowdon, while to the north, you can gaze across the Menai Straits to Anglesey and the Irish Sea.

The northern hills of the Carneddau are less frequented than their southern counterparts, and you will probably have some of their summits to yourself. It is a wild and desolate area whose rounded tops and long broad ridges, overlooking ice-carved cwms, provide wonderful walking on a grand scale when there is good visibility. In unfavourable weather conditions, good navigation skills are essential, since there are few easily identifiable features.

Bont Newydd to Garnedd Uchaf

The walk starts at Bont Newydd where a narrow road rising from Aber village crosses the Afon Rhaeadr-fawr. There are car parks either side of the bridge giving easy access to a wide, waymarked track on the east side of the river. The track climbs steadily up through ancient broad-leaved woodland – mainly oak – and grassy meadows in the Coedydd Aber National Nature Reserve, passing an interpretation centre. After about 2km/1¼ miles you arrive at the impressive cascades of Rhaeadr-fawr – usually known simply as Aber Falls - framed by a group of trees. Here the white waters of the Afon Goch tumble 37m/120 feet down an impressive black cliff of hard granophyre into a deep pool. After heavy rain, the plunging wall of water is a thrilling spectacle, with the air filled with spray and the noise of crashing water.

In summer, this immensely popular attraction usually has crowds of visitors, with children paddling in the many rocky pools. The crowds are soon left behind though as you cross the footbridge below the falls and follow a waymarked footpath – the North Wales Path - alongside a fence. The path contours to the smaller falls of Rhaeadr-bach and then continues west to cross the stream of the Afon Gam. Just beyond where the main path turns sharp right, a stile crosses a fence on the left into a picturesque valley. A faint path now weaves its way up a steep grassy spur to a dip on the skyline where a clearer path is joined. By traversing right across grassy slopes you soon arrive at the summit trig point of Moel Wnion with its fine views across to Anglesey.

Descending back south, the small peak of Gyrn, with its spoil heaps and stone shelters, is soon crossed before rejoining the main path. This ascends grassy slopes south-east towards the rounded hill of Drosgl, whose stony summit is just off the main path up to the left. From Drosgl's huge circular pile of stones, reputed to be Bronze Age in origin, you are rewarded with splendid views north across to Anglesey and south to the outlying summit of Yr Elen, backed by the crag-girted Carnedd Dafydd with the Glyderau to the right.

About a 1km/ ⅔mile to the east is Bera Bach (the little hayrick) whose summit, with its boulders and spikes of rock, is easily reached beyond a broad grassy col. From here the huge slate quarries overlooking Bethesda are clearly visible to the south-west. It's worth the slight detour out and back to the north-east across the spongy moorland to visit the slightly lower Bera Mawr (the large hayrick), from whose craggy top you can look into the hanging Cwm yr Afon Goch whose streams merge to feed Aber Falls. Apart from sheep and a few wild ponies this landscape sees few people.

Aber Falls (Rhaeadr-fawr).

Approaching Bera Bach.

Looking south-west towards Bethesda over Drosgl from Bera Bach.

Looking east from the slopes of Moel Wnion towards Foel-ganol.

INFORMATION

Start/Finish: Forestry Commission car park at Bont Newydd GR: 664719.

Distance: 18km/11 miles.

Walking Time/total climb: 6-8 hours/ 1000m (3280 feet).

Grading: Very Difficult; a high level walk through some little-visited areas. Good navigation skills needed in poor weather conditions.

Maps: OS Explorer OL17, Snowdon – Conwy Valley.

Refreshments: Pubs and cafes in Aber.

Transport: Abergwyngregyn is served by a bus route linking Bangor with Llandudno.

Back on the main footpath the next objective is Garnedd Uchaf (highest cairn), passing the isolated rocky pimple of Yr Aryg, a small outcrop of boulders and spiky rocks, beyond which grassy slopes lead gently up to the rocky summit. Pausing to look back during the ascent, the rocky twin tops of Bera Mawr and Bach stand out from the surrounding moors like Peak District or Dartmoor tors.

At Garnedd Uchaf, you join the main north-south highway across the Carneddau, linking Arber with the Ogwen Valley. This route will be very familiar to those keen walkers who have tackled the challenging Welsh 3000 footers, a gruelling 60km/37 miles traverse of all fourteen Snowdonia summits above 3000 feet/914m within a 24 hour period. Not a route for the faint-hearted. To the south, beyond a broad saddle, is the tantalising dome of Foel Grach backed by Carnedd Llewelyn and Yr Elen. If time and weather conditions permit, then an out-and-back walk to Carnedd Llewelyn might be worth that extra effort.

Garnedd Uchaf to Bont Newydd

The walk now continues north-east along a boggy path up to the summit boulder cap of Foel-fras (rough hill), at 942m/3091 feet, usually the last of the Welsh 3000ers in this direction. In addition to the trig point, there is a beautifully-constructed wall which crosses the long, wedge-shaped summit plateau. Following the line of the wall you soon meet a fence alongside which a path descends long grassy slopes to the boggy col of Bwlch y Gwryd from where steep convex slopes drop left down to the reservoir of Llyn Anafon. If weather conditions are poor then an alternative way of completing this walk is to descend to the reservoir and then follow a track along the eastern side of the Afon Anafon.

Our way though continues along the main ridge up a short rise to the bare, eroded summit of Drum, which sports a substantial burial cairn, Carnedd Penyborth-Goch. Over time, this has been hollowed out to provide a wind shelter. Ignoring a stony track dropping to the left, the top is followed where a fence line gradually descends to Carnedd y Ddelw (cairn of the idol). Beneath an ancient burial cairn here a small gold figurine was found during excavation work in the eighteenth century.

Continuing down the gently curving ridge, with Anglesey on the skyline ahead and steep slopes leading left into the Afon Anafon valley, the stony track from Drum is crossed again. Just beyond here the twisting, undulating ridge links the prominent tops of Pen Bryn-du and Yr Orsedd with the little rocky top of Foel-ganol, the final summit on the ridge.

After descending a steep gorse-covered hillside on the north side of Foel-ganol to the foot of the ridge, you join the track of the old Roman road, rising up from the Afon Conwy. The track is followed left (west) and it soon swings south to the head of a tarmac lane. All that remains now is a gentle walk down to the car park at Bont Newydd.

A view across Cwm yr Afon Goch to Garnedd Uchaf.

Bera Mawr seen from the rocky top of Bera Bach.

Cwm Eigiau seen from the slopes of Pen Llithrig y Wrach.

Walkers at the summit of Pen Llithrig y Wrach.

WALK 2 LONELY CWM EIGIAU

This splendid outing involves a high level traverse around the craggy rim of the wild and lonely Cwm Eigiau, situated on the eastern flanks of the Carneddau. The walk captures the essence of this vast, rugged landscape. As you climb out of the Conwy Valley up the narrow lane above Tal-y-Bont you can pick out the frowning bulk of Carnedd Llewelyn, rearing up above Cwm Eigiau, making you really appreciate the huge scale of these hills.

Llyn Eigiau to Carnedd Llewelyn

A good place to start the walk is at the small car park at the end of a narrow lane, 5km/3 miles south of Tal-y-Bont. By continuing along a stony track from the road head, you soon reach the jagged rent in Llyn Eigiau's dam wall from where the broad grassy north-eastern spur of Pen Llithrig y Wrach (the hill of the slippery witch) is joined near the dwelling of Hafod-y-rhiw.

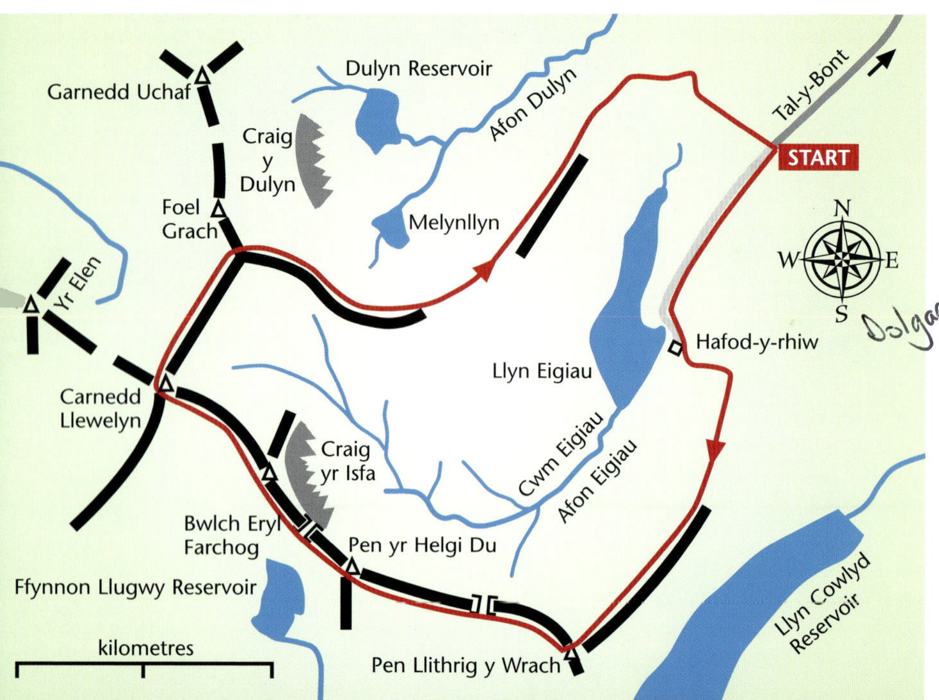

As you follow the faint path through rough moorland grass up the gradually steepening ridge, you can peer into isolated Cwm Eigiau and catch glimpses back down to the shallow sheet of water of Llyn Eigiau. The breached dam wall and Cwm Eigiau's derelict buildings are a reminder of the former mining hereabouts. On a November night in 1925, not long after the dam's construction, the wall burst and the dam's contents were spewed into Conwy, overwhelming the village and claiming sixteen lives. The dam was designed to provide power for the aluminium works at Dolgarrog. A close look at the wall explains the cause of the disaster – it was built on top of moraine debris causing it to move under pressure as the water level rose.

20

Tryfan and the Glyderau seen from the slopes of Pen Llithrig y Wrach.

From the summit of Pen Llithrig y Wrach, the first top of the day, you get excellent views across the desolate hollow of Cwm Eigiau to Carnedd Llewelyn. Having just gained all that height, some of it has now to be lost as you drop steeply to Bwlch y Tri Marchog, and then regained by a long plod up a grassy ridge to the flat-topped summit of Pen yr Helgi Du (the hill of the black hound). Grass is now replaced by rock and scree, and ahead loom the massive buttresses of Craig yr Ysfa. A plunging ridge leads excitingly down to the narrow dip of Bwlch Eryl Farchog from where you get a bird's-eye-view left down to the dark waters of Ffynnon Llugwy reservoir, its access road providing a quick approach, or an escape route in bad weather, while down the other side are the ruins of the Cwm Eigiau slate quarries, derelict since 1890.

Above left: *The view north-west to Carnedd Llewelyn from Pen yr Helgi Du.*

Above right: *Crossing Bwlch Eryl Farchog towards Craig yr Isfa.*

INFORMATION

Start/finish: Small car park at the Cwm Eigiau road head GR: 732662.
Distance: 23km/14miles.
Walking Time/total climb: 7hours/950m (3120 feet).
Grading: Very Difficult; a high level ridge walk, mainly on well-defined tracks although navigation can be difficult in misty conditions.
Maps: OS Explorer OL17.
Refreshments: Pubs and cafes in Llanrwst.
Transport: There is no public transport to this point.

At the end of the ridge, which twists across the dip for a couple of hundred metres, a short slab is reached and the start of a pleasant zig-zag scramble – which is slippery when wet and care is needed. Above the awkward slab a rocky path weaves its way up the minor top of Craig yr Ysfa, really just a sharp pinnacle on the shoulder of Carnedd Llewelyn. Despite being dwarfed by its neighbour, Craig yr Ysfa is very rugged and offers some classic rock climbs on its impressive Amphitheatre Walls.

Ahead lies a long plod up scree slopes to the summit of Carnedd Llewelyn (Llewelyn's cairn), the third highest mountain in Wales. Pause here for a well-earned breather and take in the vast panoramic views. There are no soaring ridges here, just rolling hills leading the eye round from the coast and Great Orme to Snowdon and the Glyderau. From the summit itself a series of ridges radiate out; the shortest being out and back along the arete to the shapely Yr Elen (the peak of the fawn), a hill in its own right and well worth a visit if time permits. To the south lies a broad ridge, which leads round to Carnedd Dafydd, named after one of the last Princes of Wales who welded the warring Welsh tribes into one nation. The large cairn to the north-west of Carnedd Llewelyn is said to be the burial place of Tristan, one of the Knights of the Round Table, but which more likely dates back to the Bronze Age.

Carnedd Llewelyn to Cwm Eigiau

Leaving the summit of Carnedd Llewelyn, a ridge is followed north down towards Foel Grach where, beneath a rocky knoll just north of the summit cairn, is a refuge hut. This small hut has provided protection on many occasions for walkers seeking shelter from extreme weather conditions. At the low point of a saddle just below Foel Grach, the plateau is left behind. Turning east, then south-east, you head down the wide, boggy ridge of Gledrffordd, overlooking the remote reservoirs of Dulyn and Melynllyn, the highest lake in Snowdonia.

Continuing down the broad ridge of Cefn Tal-llyn-Eigiau, keeping the dramatic rocky cliffs overlook the Eigiau reservoir to the right, you eventually arrive at the end of the ridge. By staying to the left of a high, drystone wall you descend to join a track coming in from the Melynllyn reservoir. By heading right along the track, which contours round the north-eastern spur of Craig Eigiau, you soon reach the car park and the end of a classic outing.

The entrance into Cwm Eigiau.

Crossing Craig yr Isfa on the way to Carnedd Llewelyn.

A bird's-eye-view down the cliffs of Craig yr Isfa into Cwm Eigiau.

Pen yr Ole Wen reflected in Llyn Idwal.

This popular clockwise traverse of the high plateau linking the two highest peaks of the Carneddau – Carnedd Dafydd and Carnedd Llewelyn – starts from the Ogwen Valley side of the range. The first objective is Pen yr Ole Wen which extends south from the main bulk of the Carneddau and rises steeply from the shores of Llyn Ogwen. The zigzag path up the shaly south ridge of Pen yr Ole Wen, starting from the outflow of Llyn Ogwen, is brutally steep, loose and unremitting. This walk ascends the gentler east ridge above the east end of Llyn Ogwen as a prelude to a traverse of the high Carneddau tops including an ascent of the delightful outlying peak of Yr Elen.

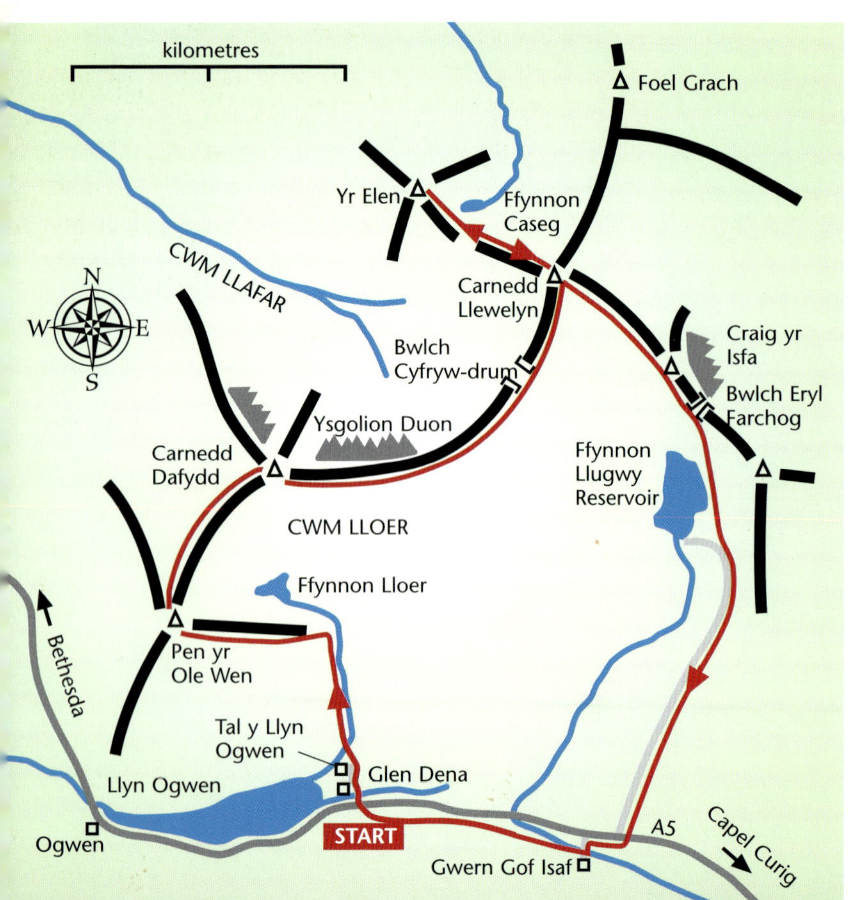

The Ogwen Valley to Carnedd Llewelyn

From Glen Dena, on the A5 road just west of Gwern Gof Uchaf Farm, a track crosses a bridge and leads to the farm at Tal y Llyn Ogwen. Just before the farm is reached, a ladder stile over a wall on the right gives access to an often boggy waymarked path which weaves its way, mainly on the west side of a stream, up towards Cwm Lloer. At the lip of the cwm is the start of the broad end of the rocky east ridge of Pen yr Ole Wen.

After some scrambling up a short gully, the path eventually winds up the crest of the ridge. From here you can look down right into the craggy and secluded ice-carved Cwm Lloer, which contains the little lake of Ffynnon Lloer (spring of the moon). The cwm also provides competent scramblers with an excellent Grade 3 route on the prominent crag of Craig Lloer, whose left edge gives a superbly exposed scramble on excellent rock – the Craig Lloer Spur. Above the cliff a broad ridge leads pleasantly up to the summit of Pen yr Ole Wen.

24

As you make progress up the east ridge of Pen yr Ole Wen you have time to appreciate the view across the Ogwen Valley to the wedge-shaped Tryfan and the rocky peaks of the Glyderau.   From the summit of Pen yr Ole Wen a broad ridge rises north-east around the rim of Cwm Lloer towards Carnedd Dafydd (Dafydd's cairn), passing over the minor top of Carnedd Fach with its huge mound of stones.

A steady climb now leads to the summit of Carnedd Dafydd (1044m/3412 feet) crowned by a heap of stones and a three-sided windbreak set in a rocky wilderness. After the long climb the summit is a great place to stop for a break and take in the views, especially east across the vast Carneddau plateau. Heading south-west a well-worn path leads around the rim of the vast broken and vegetated cliffs of Ysgolion Duon (the black ladders), forming a huge cirque below the summit of Carnedd Dafydd. Here steep gullies plunge impressively into the depths of Cwm Llafar.

Descending from Bwlch Eryl Farchog to Ffynnon Llugwy Reservoir.

Tryfan seen from the slopes of Pen yr Ole Wen.

Walkers heading for Carnedd Llewelyn.

A view over Craig yr Isfa to Pen yr Helgi Du.

Craig yr Isfa's cliffs dominate the view from Bwlch Eryl Farchog.

Across Cwm Llafar you can pick out the shapely brow of the outlying peak of Yr Elen, linked to Carnedd Llewelyn by a narrow ridge. From here you also have dramatic views of Anglesey and back across the Ogwen Valley to the rocky cwms of the Glyderau. The path follows a ridge north-east across Bwlch Cyfryw-drum, becoming much narrower before climbing up towards Carnedd Llewelyn (Llewelyn's cairn). A final trudge up a rocky slope lands you at a large cairn and windbreaks on the plateau-like summit, at 1064m/3491feet, the third highest Welsh peak.

From here there are rolling hills in all directions backed by fine panoramic views, stretching from Carnedd Dafydd and the Snowdon range round to the coast and Great Orme. From the summit of Carnedd Llewelyn, four ridges radiate out, the longest one stretching to the north-east towards Drum, with the shortest being out along to Yr Elen (the peak of the fawn), one of the shapeliest peaks in the Carneddau.

If time permits then an out-and-back detour to Yr Elen is highly recommended. Heading north-west across the summit plateau you reach a path descending along a narrow and exposed ridge to the rocky summit of Yr Elen. Here you have an excellent view across Cwm Llafar to the cliffs of the Black Ladders. Down to the right, situated in a sheltered, craggy cwm is the beautifully situated tiny lake of Fynnon Caseg, above which a sharp ridge soars up round the northern edge of the cwm to the top of Yr Elen.

Carnedd Llewelyn to the Ogwen Valley

Retracing your steps back to Carnedd Llewelyn, a path now descends south-east. In anything but clear conditions, it's worth setting a compass bearing for the descent. Scree slopes lead down to a rockier section along the rim of Cwm Eigiau where the path weaves its way around rocks and boulders towards Craig yr Ysfa. Beyond this minor summit, the path plunges down broken, polished rocks, which require care in windy, wet or winter conditions. At the foot of this awkward section you arrive at the narrow, grassy and exposed col of Bwlch Eryl Farchog, linking Craig yr Ysfa with Pen yr Helgi Du. Down to the left is Cwm Eigiau and the impressive cliffs of Craig yr Ysfa, while down to the right is Ffynnon Llugwy Reservoir.

From the lowest point of the dip a path traverses steeply south via a series of zigzags to eventually arrive at the shore of Ffynnon Llugwy, from where a metalled access road leads easily down to the A5, accompanied by great views along the Ogwen Valley. Just along the road to the right a farm track to Gwern Gof Isaf – a popular campsite – leads left. From here the track of the old Ogwen Valley road can be followed across fields below the impressive east face of Tryfan, rejoining the A5 opposite Glen Dena.

Right: *Approaching Carnedd Dafydd, with Carnedd Llewelyn in the background.*

Below: *A winter view of Cwm Lloer from the Ogwen Valley.*

INFORMATION

Start/Finish: Glen Dena Bridge, Ogwen Valley GR: 668606. Various road-side car parks.

Distance: 14.5km/9 miles

Walking Time/total climb: 6hours/808m (2650 feet).

Grading: Very Difficult; a high-level walk on mainly reasonable paths but with the option of a scrambling ascent of the Craig Lloer Spur; good navigation skills needed in poor weather conditions.

Maps: OS Explorer OL17.

Refreshments: Kiosk at the Ogwen Cottage car park, pubs and cafes in Capel Curig and Bethesda.

Transport: Regular bus service between Bethesda and Betwys-y-Coed.

2 TRYFAN AND THE GLYDERAU

The hills overlooking the Ogwen Valley (more correctly known as Nant y Benglog) offer some of the finest and most dramatic walking in Snowdonia. Travelling west along the A5 Holyhead road, who can forget their first view of the wedge-shaped Tryfan, especially when it is lit up by early morning sunshine. Its shape is instantly recognizable and provides one of the great sights in the British hills. Summer or winter its geometrical symmetry draws walkers and climbers back time and time again. Beyond Tryfan are a series of spectacular north facing ice-scalloped cwms, soaring ridges and the brooding cliffs of Glyder Fach and Glyder Fawr. On Ogwen's south facing flanks are the rolling whaleback hills of the Carneddau and to the west of Llyn Ogwen is the glacial trough of the Nant Ffrancon.

The name Y Glyderau – known to generations of English-speaking walkers simply as 'the Glyders' – usually refers to the whole group of peaks on the long and twisting spine of craggy hills stretching in a north-easterly arc from Carnedd y Filiast, overlooking Bethesda, to Gallt yr Ogof near Capel Curig with Cwm Idwal at its heart. The Glyderau are bounded to the north by the Ogwen Valley and the Nant Ffrancon, and to the south by Llanberis Pass. Just off the main spine, but linked by fine ridges, lie Elidir Fawr and the incomparable Tryfan.

The Glyderau provide a feast of paths and narrow ridges to choose from, although they should not be underestimated in bad weather, especially under snow. There are plenty of

Tryfan seen from the outflow of Llyn Ogwen.

Reflections of Foel Goch in Llyn Ogwen.

Evening light on Tryfan and the Glyderau.

Feral goats on Tryfan.

Scrambling on Glyder Fawr above Cwm Idwal.

Mist rises from Foel Goch.

parking lay-bys spread throughout the Ogwen Valley to provide numerous starting points for a day on these hills. Even on wet days there are some interesting low-level walks, such as around Llyn Ogwen, or into Cwm Idwal, where you can absorb the atmosphere of this wonderful place.

Most of the summits of this grand range can be visited on a long skyline walk of 20km (12 miles) from Capel Curig to Bethesda. But then you would miss out on the many delights to be found in the rocky cwms with their airy ridges and mountain lakes (llyns) such as Llyn Bochlwyd, Llyn Idwal and shy Llyn Clyd, cradled in the twin east ridges of Y Garn, whose familiar bulk dominates the view beyond Llyn Ogwen.

Below: *Y Garn from the shore of Llyn Idwal.*

Tryfan reflected in a small, un-named lake on Glyder Fach.

Tryfan dominates the view down the Ogwen Valley.

You need numerous visits before these craggy cwms give up their hidden secrets, like the tiny unnamed lake surrounded by crags and hidden high up in the back of Cwm Bochlwyd. You might even be lucky and catch a glimpse of the elusive herd of feral goats which roam Tryfan's craggy slopes. You will certainly be able to look down on noisy, low-flying RAF jets as they scream through the Ogwen Valley – a regular weekday occurrence.

Tryfan and the Glyderau are also a mecca for climbers and scramblers, and the combination of Tryfan's North Ridge followed by Glyder Fach's Bristly Ridge is one of the classic outings in Snowdonia and should be on every experienced walker's and scrambler's itinerary.

Due to a lack of accommodation in the Ogwen Valley – two campsites and a youth hostel (Idwal Cottage) – Capel Curig, Bethesda and Betws-y-Coed are the usual bases for exploring the area. There are numerous hotels, B&Bs and campsites in these villages. For car users access is easy and public transport is provided by the Snowdon Sherpa bus service, which runs through the valley, connecting Bethesda, Capel Curig and Betws-y-Coed which also provides a link with the national rail network.

Looking down the North Ridge of Tryfan to Llyn Ogwen.

Tryfan is one of the few hills in Snowdonia where you have to use your hands as well as feet to reach the summit. There are several ways of approaching the famous obelisks of Adam and Eve which crown Tryfan's top, the easiest being up its south ridge via Cwm Bochlwyd to the west or Cwm Tryfan to the east. But for adventurous walkers who like some easy scrambling, there is only one way – the North Ridge.

The North Ridge rises uncompromisingly from the roadside at Llyn Ogwen to the summit of Tryfan (the pointed peak) and provides arguably the most direct and entertaining way up any mountain in all Wales. There are crags, gullies and rocky ridges at every turn to provide challenges for scramblers, although most of the difficulties can easily be bypassed. The continuation along the pinnacles of Bristly Ridge to the summit of Glyder Fach maintains the mountaineering atmosphere of the trip, as does the rocky descent beside the Devil's Kitchen into Cwm Idwal. In winter this outing, especially Bristly Ridge, takes on a truly Alpine character.

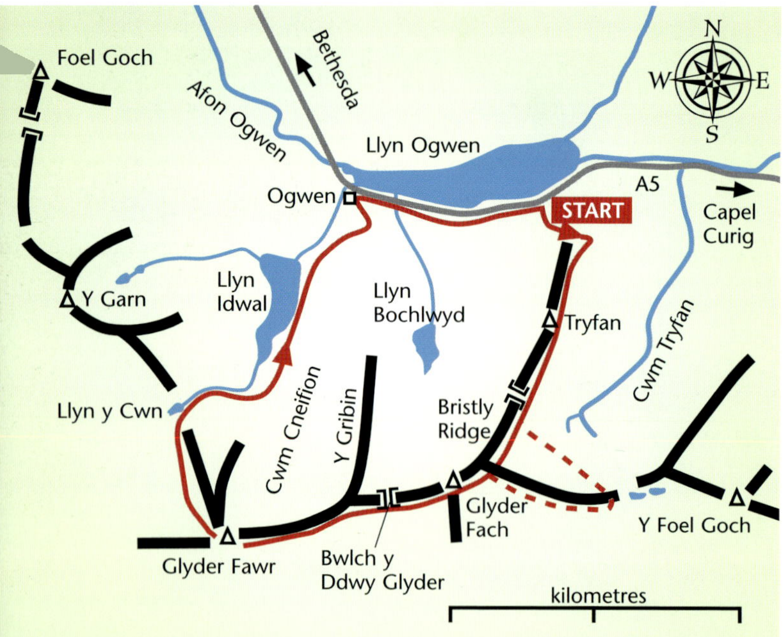

Milestone Buttress to Tryfan

The walk starts at the road below the Milestone Buttress, named because of its position above the tenth milestone – long since gone – on the A5 road from Bangor. From a lay-by, a stile gives access to a path and rocky steps alongside a wall, which is followed up towards Milestone Buttress, trending left round the side of the cliffs. The buttresses here have given a rock-climbing introduction to generations of beginners.

Steep scree and boulder slopes eventually lead up to a heathery shoulder where a network of paths cross. The path for Heather Terrace, another interesting way up Tryfan, passing below its east buttresses and gullies, sneaks off left, while the broad, easy angled North Ridge lies up scree paths to the right.

Staying on the left side of the ridge you can follow worn paths up rocky terrain which is never technically difficult, but there are sometimes route-finding problems. At a distinct step in the ridge is the famous landmark of the Cannon, an inclined slab of rock which is prominent from the western side of Tryfan. The route continues to the left up walls, chimneys and arêtes, taking up the challenges as they arrive. You select the difficulties up the scratched rock, or avoid them as the mood takes you. Towards the top the ridge narrows, a final short wall requiring care followed by a descent into a notch. Climbing out of the notch, a final scramble over delightful rock soon lands you at the north summit.

The central, and highest summit, at 915m/3002 feet, is just a short distance ahead, easily identified by the twin monoliths known as Adam and Eve. According to tradition, if you make the risky step across from the top of one block to the other, you are deemed to have received the freedom of Tryfan. However, a word of warning; the tops of the blocks have become very polished and slippery, and the steep drop down the east face is only a short distance away.

Despite Tryfan's close proximity to higher peaks, its summit, set far above the brooding depths of the Ogwen Valley, is quite aloof. You have excellent views across Llyn Ogwen to the vast Carneddau range filling the northern skyline. But the best views are of the Glyderau and especially into Llyn Bochlwyd and Llyn Idwal backed by the elegant peak of Y Garn.

Tryfan to Glyder Fach

Tryfan's undulating rocky but easy south ridge is now descended, turning any difficulties on the western side. Eventually a path curves round to the left to reach Bwlch Tryfan. Bristly Ridge, linking Tryfan with Glyder Fach, lies straight ahead and is reached by following a footpath alongside a stone wall up to the foot of the ridge.

Though no harder than Tryfan's North Ridge, Bristly Ridge is much narrower and more direct with pinnacles and steep drops all around. This exposed ridge is one of the most popular scrambles in Snowdonia, as can be seen from the scratched rock

The east face of Tryfan catches the early morning sunshine.

Typical craggy terrain on Tryfan's North Ridge.

Approaching Tryfan's summit.

Above: *Tryfan reflected in Llyn y Caseg-fraith on the east ridge of Glyder Fach.*

Left: *High on Bristly Ridge.*

making the route easy to follow. From the foot of the ridge a dark gully gives access to the ridge proper and the start of an exhilarating traverse over pinnacles with the descent into the obvious Great Gap being the hardest section. The ridge ends above a series of pinnacles from where easier terrain leads up to the summit plateau of Glyder Fach at 994m/3261 feet.

If Bristly Ridge doesn't appeal, then you can traverse left from Bwlch Tryfan and follow the upper section of the Miners' Track, across the head of Cwm Tryfan to join the east ridge of Glyder Fach near Llyn y Caseg-fraith. Glyder Fach's rocky east ridge is then ascended to the rocky summit, which lies near the top of Bristly Ridge.

Castell y Gwynt (castle of the winds) backed by Glyder Fawr.

Descending the north-east slopes of Glyder Fawr to Llyn y Cwn backed by Y Garn.

INFORMATION
Start/Finish: Several car parks below Milestone Buttress. GR: 663603.
Distance: 9.5km/7 miles.
Walking Time/total climb: 6-8 hours/ 950m (3100 feet).
Grading: Very Difficult; a long mountain day, which involves some easy scrambling with exposed situations on the Bristly Ridge. A serious outing in bad weather conditions, especially when the hills are snow-covered.
Maps: OS Explorer OL17.
Refreshments: Kiosk at the Ogwen Cottage car park, pubs and cafes in Capel Curig and Bethesda.
Transport: Regular bus service between Bethesda and Betwys-y-Coed.

The word Glyder, is thought to derive from the Celtic word *cludr*, a 'heap or pile of stones', which is quite appropriate for this splintered rocky wonderland around the summit of Glyder Fach (lesser heap). This is nature in the raw. The nearby Cantilever Slab, a special favourite of photographers, has stood the test of time and has refused to tip over despite the numerous people who have balanced on its crest. Thomas Pennant is credited with its first ascent in 1781.

Glyder Fach to Ogwen Cottage

From the chaotic jumble of rocks at the top of Glyder Fach it is only a short descent west to Castell y Gwynt (castle of the winds), an impressive rocky outcrop of tall spikes and blocks situated between the two Glyderau and arranged like the ruins of an ancient castle. You can either scramble directly over the serrated skyline or sneak round the slabby rocks on the left. Coming up from the right, just beyond Castell y Gwynt, is the ridge of Y Gribin, another escape route which offers a steep descent to Lyn Bochlwyd.

Ahead the broad, heavily-cairned whaleback ridge rises steadily to the top of Glyder Fawr (greater heap) at 999m/3278 feet, the highest point on the Glyderau ridge. However, in misty weather you might have trouble finding the actual summit in the numerous outcrops of sharp, spiky flakes scattered among the vast stony dome. On clear crisp days you are rewarded by one of the finest prospects in North Wales, stretching from the smooth Carneddau to the jagged crests of Snowdon beyond Llanberis Pass, while south on the distant horizon lie Cadair Idris and the peaks of the Arenig, Aran and Rhinogau.

At Glyder Fawr the crest turns north-west and steep screes plunge down to a wide grassy col which cradles the small lake of Llyn y Cwn (the lake of the hounds) whose waters tumble down the great cleft of Twll Du (the Devil's kitchen) into Llyn Idwal. About 150m/500 feet before the lake is reached, a cairned path can be followed right, down a shallow stony gully steeply into Cwm Idwal, traversing below steep cliffs in the amphitheatre of Twll Du. This place has an air of mystery about it and often shows a moody intensity, especially when the clouds are low and grey mists swirl around the steep damp cliffs; Idwal's storm clouds are supposed to be brewed up in this cauldron.

After scrambling through a mass of boulders the path bears right, passing below Idwal Slabs, a place redolent with the history of Welsh rock climbing and a popular place for beginners. Beyond the slabs the path continues along the east side of Llyn Idwal and down to Ogwen Cottage from where the A5 is followed back to the start.

Below left: *Crossing the pinnacles on Bristly Ridge.*

Bottom left: *The exposed step between the Adam and Eve obelisks.*

Below right: *The Cantilever near Glyder Fach's summit.*

The shapely peak of Y Garn.

Y GARN AND THE WEST WALL OF THE NANT FFRANCON

This high-level circuit, starting from Ogwen Cottage, follows a series of peaks from Y Garn to Carnedd y Filiast linked by a fine ridge and overlooking the steep, rocky cwms, which form the west wall of the Nant Ffrancon. It is also a much quieter walk than the ever-popular ridges on Glyder Fach and Glyder Fawr.

Y Garn (the cairn) is an elegant mountain, which dominates the Ogwen Valley, arguably more so than the wedge-shaped Tryfan. In fact Y Garn is best seen from high up on the north ridge of Tryfan from where it gives the appearance of a comfortable armchair overlooking Llyn Idwal. Two fine curving ridges – the arms of the chair – sweep down to enclose a hanging cwm, Cwm Clyd, carved out by glacial action and containing a couple of exquisite lakes known by the single name of Llyn Clyd; this place is one of the hidden gems of Ogwen.

Ogwen Cottage to Y Garn

Y Garn is approached from Ogwen Cottage up a broad track leading to the west end of Llyn Idwal from where the two main ridges sweeping down to Llyn Idwal are to be seen. You have a choice of routes here. The left-hand ridge (the east ridge) offers some easy scrambling in its lower section but is blocked high up by a crag – Castell y Geifr (castle of the goat) – straddling the ridge. To overcome this involves some Grade 2 scrambling up its left side followed by an ascent of a steep wall rearing up beyond a rocky gap. A grassy ridge then sweeps up to the summit.

The right hand ridge encircling Cwm Clyd is much more attractive for walkers – though still steep – and is a very popular way up Y Garn as can be seen by the eroded path and polished rocks. From a gateway in a wall at the foot of the ridge, an initial steep rise up the rocky hillside leads to a shoulder overlooking the two small lakes in Cwm Clyd, with fine views down the Nant Ffrancon and into Cwm Idwal. From here the path swings south-west up to the top of Y Garn, its summit at 947m/3106 feet, adorned with a low circular stone shelter. This is a welcome place for refreshments and to take in the splendid panoramic views especially across Cwm Idwal to Glyder Fach and Tryfan.

Y Garn to Ogwen

The walk now continues more easily north along a gritty path down to a minor dip at the lowest point on the rim of Cwm Cywion. Easy grassy slopes beside a fence lead over a little bump up to Foel Goch (the red hill), the actual summit at 947m/3106 feet, being up to the right of the main path. The grassy western flanks of Foel Goch are in marked contrast to the impressive Cwm-coch, which bites deeply into its eastern flanks. Here, two steep ridges overlook the cwm – the left-bounding bristling crags of Creigiau Gleison and the soaring right-hand ridge of Yr Esgair, a ridge so clearly seen on the skyline from Llyn Ogwen.

After descending steeply from Foel Goch the path drops down to the grassy Bwlchy Brecan then continues north up beside a fence to the grassy summit of Mynydd Perfedd (middle mountain), at 813m/2667feet. This is an unim-pressive hill apart from the view west to the elegant, cone-shaped Elidir Fawr.

A recommended detour out and back south-west from Mynydd Perfedd also allows a visit to the summit of Elidir Fawr (great cairn of Elidir), at 920m/3018 feet one of the Welsh 3000 footers. The walk involves following a ridge either side of a dip at Bwlych y Marchlyn, curving high above the shimmering waters of Marchlyn Mawr Reservoir and the imposing Pillar of Elidir rising from the scree slopes above the southern shoreline.

Right: *Easy scrambling on the East Ridge of Y Garn, with Llyn Idwal and Llyn Ogwen clearly visible.*

The final slopes to the summit of Y Garn, with Tryfan in the background.

A winter view of Foel Goch across Llyn Ogwen.

Dawn light illuminates Foel Goch.

Marchlyn Mawr Reservoir supplies water to the Dinorwig pumped-storage power station in the valley below. At off-peak times water is pumped from Llyn Peris back up to the higher lake and then released to drop through the mountain, turning underground turbines to generate electricity during the day when demand is high. This lowers the water level in the reservoir by 35m/105 feet creating a tide-mark around its edge. There is a fascinating 'Electric Mountain' exhibition centre on the shore of Lake Padarn in Llanberis and there are also organised tours of the generating station.

Back at Mynydd Perfedd a spacious grassy saddle now stretches north to Carnedd y Filiast (cairn of the greyhound bitch), at 822m/2697 feet, the last summit on the walk. The gentle, grassy termination of the main ridge belies the fact that the eastern slopes of Carnedd y Filiast fall into the remote Cwm Graianog, the north side of which is dominated by a huge expanse of overlapping slabs over 200m/650 feet high and known locally as Creigiau's Rowlar. From the lip of Cwm Graianog you get an excellent view across the huge, rippled Atlantic Slab, with its numerous veins of conspicuous white quartzite running across the surface.

Continuing north along the ridge from Carnedd y Filiast, a faint path descends towards the vast Penryhn slate quarries overlooking Bethesda. Further down the ridge, a path is joined which traverses down right into Cwm Ceunant before dropping to join the old Nant Ffrancon road. The road is then followed right, past the farm at Maes-Caradoc. As you approach Ogwen Cottage you also have a view of the cascades of Rhaeadr Ogwen (Ogwen Falls) with the rugged hills of the Ogwen Valley providing a magnificent backdrop.

INFORMATION
Start/Finish: Ogwen Cottage car park
GR: 649604.
Distance: 15km/9.5 miles.
Walking Time/total climb: 7 hours/
1039m (3409 feet).
Grading: Very Difficult; a high level walk
on mainly good paths and with the option of
a scrambling route on Y Garn.
Maps: OS Explorer OL17.
Refreshments: Kiosk at the Ogwen
Cottage car park and pubs and cafés in Capel
Curig and Bethesda.
Transport: Regular bus service between
Bethesda and Betwys-y-Coed.

The west wall of the Nant Ffrancon seen from Pen yr Ole Wen.

Crossing the rocky gap and crag on the East Ridge of Y Garn.

The shapely and graceful peak of Elidir Fawr.

Looking across the head wall of Cwm Idwal.

This fascinating walk around Cwm Idwal's rocky skyline, taking in Glyder Fawr and Y Garn, is an ideal way to really appreciate the scale, drama and geology of this dramatic cwm. One of the highlights of the walk is a view from Y Garn into the craggy depths of Cwm Idwal backed by the familiar profile of Tryfan.

Cwm Idwal, a National Nature Reserve, is situated in the heart of the Glyderau, and is justly famous for its dramatic beauty, superb scrambling and rock climbing, botany and especially its geology. Charles Darwin, who visited the cwm in 1841, was the first to recognise that Idwal's scenery was entirely the work of glaciers. All the signs of ice action are here: smoothed rocks; perched erratic boulders deposited by receding glaciers; an archetypal moraine-dammed hollow; and hillocks which are fine examples of 'roches moutonees', planed off on their eastern sides by a giant glacier which gouged its way down the Ogwen Valley and Nant Ffrancon towards the Irish Sea.

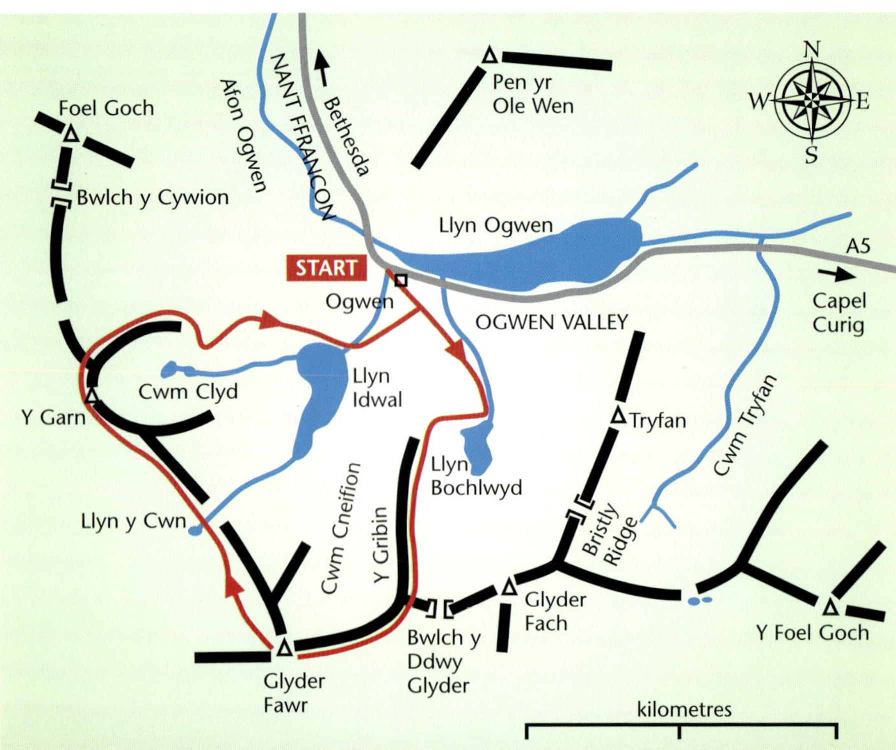

When you visit the cwm for the first time you cannot fail to be impressed by the sheer scale of one of the finest vistas in Wales: a glacial cirque enclosing the dark waters of Llyn Idwal, and surrounded on three sides by dramatic mountains. The head of the cwm is a twisted mass of cliffs and ravines and here is found one of Britain's finest examples of a huge downfold of rock – the Idwal syncline. You could spend hours here exploring the cwm and its lake backed by the broad sweep of Idwal Slabs, at the foot of huge grey cliffs which lead the eye up to Glyder Fawr and right round to the deep cleft of the Devil's Kitchen and bulky Y Garn.

Y Garn seen to the west from the top of Y Gribin.

The approach to Idwal Slabs alongside Llyn Idwal.

Ogwen Cottage to Glyder Fawr

From Ogwen Cottage, a constructed path leads up left of the snack bar and soon crosses a footbridge over the outflow from Llyn Idwal. Ignoring the right turn into Cwm Idwal, you continue straight ahead via the Miners' Track, initially over easy but damp grassy terrain, before climbing steeply up a well-constructed rocky stairway. The path rises above the ravine of Nant Bochlwyd to the shores of Llyn Bochlwyd, one of the most enchanting of Snowdonia's lakes.

Llyn Bochlwyd is a great place to pause for a breather and take in the tremendous views of the craggy west face of Tryfan and the northern skyline across the Ogwen Valley, which is filled by the shapely cone of Pen yr Ole Wen and the gentle undulating spine of the Carneddau. The main cliff of Glyder Fach, with its sheer pillars and walls of grey rock split by cracks and corners, sits high above Llyn Bochlwyd and is bounded on the east by Bristly Ridge, and to the west by Y Gribin. These dramatic cliffs have been popular with generations of climbers.

An erratic boulder in Cwm Idwal.

Eroded rocks near the summit of Glyder Fawr.

Our way now lies up the obvious, soaring ridge of Y Gribin on the right-hand side of the cwm sweeping down to the lake and separating Cwm Bochlywd from its neighbour Cwm Cneifion. From the northern point of Llyn Bochlwyd a path wends its way up the broad grassy ridge, easy at first but eventually rising steeply up a narrow crest to land you on an open plateau of smooth, short-cropped grass.

The character of the ridge now changes, its smooth turf being replaced by scree slopes, which sweep up to the foot of a steep rocky ridge. Although most difficulties can be avoided by an eroded path, which weaves its way up between small crags up the right side of the ridge, the actual crest provides some entertaining scrambling (Grade 1). Never really too technical, the situation is certainly exhilarating and experienced hill walkers and scramblers will relish the exposed situations high above Cwm Bochlwyd. You also get a stunning perspective of Tryfan.

Suddenly the scrambling is all over and you arrive at the cairn on the bouldery plateau between the two Glyderau a short distance from Castell y Gwynt (the castle of the winds), a stark rocky outcrop with slabs and pillars arranged like the ruins of an ancient castle. A broad ridge now rises up right to Glyder Fawr (greater heap), at 999m/3278 feet, the highest point on the Glyderau ridge. In misty conditions it is not always easy to find the actual summit among the numerous outcrops scattered across this vast stony dome. On clear crisp days though you are rewarded by one of the finest panoramic views in North Wales.

Heading up the summit ridge to Glyder Fawr with Castell y Gwynt in the background.

Glyder Fawr to Ogwen

At Glyder Fawr the crest turns north-west and steep screes sweep down to a wide grassy col which holds the small lake of Llyn y Cwn (the lake of the hounds) whose waters tumble down the great cleft of Twll Du (the Devil's kitchen) into Llyn Idwal. If you wish, the walk can be shortened from here by following a cairned track steeply into Cwm Idwal via the amphitheatre of Twll Du.

Ice-covered rocks on Glyder Fawr.

Ahead lies the next objective on the round, the dome of Y Garn (the cairn), which is approached by a good path which initially is easy going but ends with a steep pull up to the stony summit windbreak at 947m/3107 feet. The panoramic views are worth it though, especially south-west to the Snowdon range and across Cwm Idwal to Tryfan and the cwms and craggy ridges of the Glyderau, with the dark waters of Llyn Ogwen to the left.

The descent route is the steep ridge, which wraps itself round the northern flanks of Llyn Clyd to eventually arrive at the shores of Llyn Idwal where you can enjoy the celebrated view across to Idwal Slabs and the huge cliffs of Glyder Fawr. You might want to explore some of the geological features hereabouts or, for walkers with a botanical interest, look out for the rare Snowdon lily, red campion, purple saxifrage or mountain sorrel. From a gate at the northern end of Llyn Idwal, a wide constructed track leads down to Ogwen Cottage.

Scrambling up the final rocks at the top of Y Gribin.

Crossing the dip between Y Garn and Glyder Fawr with Pen yr Ole Wen and the Carneddau visible in the background.

INFORMATION
Start/Finish: Ogwen Cottage car park, GR: 649604.
Distance: 9km/5.5miles.
Walking Time/total climb: 6-7 hours/ 961m (3153 feet).
Grading: Difficult; high level ridge walking with one section of scrambling. A serious outing in bad weather conditions, especially when the hills are snow-covered.
Maps: OS Explorer OL17.
Refreshments: Kiosk at the Ogwen Cottage car park and pubs and cafés in Capel Curig and Bethesda.
Transport: Regular bus service between Bethesda and Betwys-y-Coed.

A sea of mist surrounds the summit of Yr Wyddfa (Snowdon).

Storms sweep across Cwm Dyli on the eastern flanks of Snowdon.

3   THE SNOWDON RANGE

Few sights are more compelling than that of the Snowdon range at dawn on a windless morning reflected in the mirror-like surface of Llynnau Mymbyr near Capel Curig. The compact Snowdon massif with its sharp, rocky peaks including Yr Wyddfa, the highest summit at 1085m/3560 feet, contains some of the most magnificent mountains south of Scotland. The range has six major ridges, three of them radiating directly out from the central peak of Yr Wyddfa. These ridges also enclose wild and craggy cwms, two of which contain the finest cliffs in North Wales – Clogwyn Du'r Arddu and Y Lliwedd.

The name 'Snowdon' really covers the whole mountain massif including the summits of Yr Wyddfa, Carnedd Ugain – the second highest mountain in Wales and England – Y Lliwedd and Crib Goch. Carnedd Ugain is also shown as Garnedd Ugain on some maps. The Welsh name Yr Wyddfa, applying just to Snowdon's final summit pyramid, means 'the tomb' or 'the burial mound', although any evidence of an ancient grave which might have once existed here has vanished. Some legends ascribe the tomb to Rhita, a mythological giant slain by King Arthur.

Snowdon's top is really a curved ridge about 0.8km/½ mile long with a dip in the middle; at one end is Yr Wyddfa and at the other Carnedd Ugain (cairn of the twenty). Walkers usually refer to Carnedd Ugain as Crib y Ddysgl (crest of the dish), but this is really the name of the ridge overlooking Cwm Glas. From this main summit ridge, subsidiary ridges with their own tops spread out from both ends and provide some excellent approaches to Snowdon.

Not surprisingly, Snowdon, Wales' pre-eminent peak, with its summit café, railway from Llanberis and numerous constructed footpaths, is a very popular mountain, especially during the summer months and bank holidays. Since Victorian times an ascent of Snowdon has been a popular tourist activity. The first recorded ascent of Snowdon was by the botanist, Thomas Johnson, in 1639 but it was the

The main Snowdon peaks seen across Cwm Dyli.

The Snowdon range reflected in Llynnau Mymbyr near Capel Curig. A classic view.

opening of Telford's London to Holyhead road (A5) in 1815 and the Llanberis Pass road in 1830 which made Snowdon much more accessible. By 1847 a small collection of wooden huts had been built around the summit, one of them being known as the Roberts' Hotel after the proprietor and respected guide John Roberts.

With the arrival in 1896 of the Snowdon Mountain Railway from Llanberis, along with a café and terminus just below the summit of Snowdon, a new phase began. This rack and pinion railway runs for 8km/5 miles from Llanberis to the summit of Yr Wyddfa. It has operated since its official opening at Easter in 1896, an event which culminated in the railway's only fatal accident following a locomotive derailment. Today diesel traction rubs shoulders with steam engines, whose smoke is often visible from many of the hills in the National Park. Walkers may have mixed views about the facility – as with the new funicular railway up Cairngorm in Scotland – but it does at least allow many people who would never be able to walk up to the summit to appreciate the unique views.

Snowdon's summit café, originally built of wood, was replaced in 1936 by the present concrete-clad structure, designed by the renowned architect Sir Clough Williams-Ellis, of Portmeirion fame. Despite numerous attempts over the years to improve the bunker-like café – a major eyesore to many – approval was given in January 2004 for an ambitious multi-million pound refurbishment project to upgrade the building over the next couple of years. The Snowdon Summit Project will involve replacing the present building with a lower, more environmentally-friendly structure which blends in with the natural rocks of the summit.

At present more than 350,000 walkers and train passengers visit the summit, café and its facilities each year. With these numbers you can see why so much work has had to be carried out by the National Park Authority to renovate eroded footpaths. Much of this difficult work has been carried out in as natural way as possible to blend in with the surrounding terrain. The pitched path which has replaced the once-notorious zigzags of the Miners' Track up the steep slopes above Cwm Glaslyn, is an excellent example of this work.

Glaslyn and Lliwedd seen from the slopes of Carnedd Ugain.

Crossing Crib Goch's narrow ridge.

Ascending Crib y Ddysgl.

Llyn Glas and Clogwyn y Person.

Enclosed in a triangle by the roads linking Beddgelert, Caernarfon and Pen y Gwryd, there are various access points to the range including Llanberis, Pen-y-Pass, Bethania near Beddgelert, Rhyd Ddu and the Snowdon Ranger. There are regular bus services from Betwys-y-Coed, Llanberis, Bangor and Caernarfon, and in the summer months regular Snowdon Sherpa buses go round the range, which means you do not have to start and end the walk at the same place. With eleven distinct tops over 610m/2000 feet and with numerous starting points, walkers are spoilt for choice. Not only do all the walking routes pass through dramatic scenery, but there are rare flowers to be seen, ruined copper mines, old slate quarries, amazing geology and links with Arthurian legends.

There are eight main ways up Snowdon, with many variations to the walks. The easiest and most popular is the Llanberis Path – also known as the Tourist Path – following the course of the Snowdon Mountain Railway. It is a safe descent route in bad weather but in icy conditions, the upper reaches of the path can be dangerous. Other popular routes are the P.Y.G. Track and Miners' Track, which both start at Pen-y-Pass, and the Snowdon Ranger Path, thought to be the oldest route. The prettiest way though is probably the Watkin Path from wooded Nantgwynant.

However, the classic route up Snowdon, starting and finishing at Pen-y-Pass, just has to be the Snowdon Horseshoe, arguably the most famous ridge scramble in Britain, which many will find quite challenging. For many walkers a crossing of Crib Goch's exposed pinnacles is a rite of passage into the world of scrambling. However, in mist or under a covering of snow and ice, all the above routes can become serious outings.

Whichever approach you use to reach Snowdon's summit, the effort is worthwhile if only for the magnificent, panoramic views. On a clear day these extend to the Presli Hills, the Wicklow Mountains of Ireland, and the Lake District, while nearer at hand you can pick out most of the groups of hills in Snowdonia, as well as Anglesey and the Irish Sea.

Left: *Lliwedd in its snowy mantle.*

Right: *Crossing the Crib Goch pinnacles.*

Bottom right: *Snowdon and Liwedd seen f rom Crib y Ddysgl.*

Below: *The steep north-east face of Snowdon sweeping up from Glaslyn. A popular venue for winter mountaineers.*

WALK 7 SNOWDON'S BIG DIPPER

The long ridge extending north-west from the summit of Snowdon and terminating at Moel Eilio gives the longest and certainly one of the most appealing ways to climb Snowdon. From Moel Eilio, high above Llanberis, this big-dipper outing involves mainly easy walking over broad grassy ridges and crosses the tops of Foel Gron, Foel Goch and Moel Cynghorion from where you have excellent views. The undulating ridge involves some big drops and re-ascents resulting in a total climb of over 1500m/5000 feet to reach the reigning peak of Yr Wyffda. The return leg is via the usually deserted ridge high above Nant Peris and the southern flanks of Llanberis Pass.

Llanberis to Moel Cynghorion

The walk starts from near the Royal Victoria Hotel with a steep road climb west out of Llanberis up Fford Capel. Passing the youth hostel on the left, the road winds up the hillside to end at a gate where you meet an old track leading over Bwlch Maesgwm to Rhyd Ddu. Just along the track to the right, an obvious way leads left up a field to a stile and the start of the long ascent up the broad north-west ridge sweeping down from Moel Eilio (Eilio's hill). A wall initially clings to the ridge, with cross walls passed over by stiles, before rough grassy pastures alongside a wire fence lead up by Braich y Foel to the summit of Moel Eilio (726m/2382 feet) and the nearby stone windbreak.

From the summit you can gaze north-east across Llanberis to the tremendous Dinorwig slate quarries, with their terraces and spoil heaps rising up towards Elidir Fawr. To the right are the Glyderau, with the shapely wedge of Tryfan peeping over the shoulder of Glyder Fach, and further right the summit dome of Snowdon looks a long, long way beyond the grassy

52

ridge ahead. The scene south is in marked contrast with the gentle, whalebacked Mynnyd Mawr and the Nantlle hills rising from a green, wooded valley, with the shapely peak of Moel Hebog in the distance.

The way is now south down a path over springy, short-cropped grass along the lip of ridge passing the two dips of Bwlch Gwyn and Bwlch Cwm Cesig, before climbing up to a cairn on Foel Gron. Along this section you can peer left down the shattered ribs, gullies and steep red screes of Cwm yr Hafod and Cwm Cesig to the small Llyn Dwythwch, while down to the right the larger Llyn Cwellyn gradually comes into view. Beyond another small descent to a grassy col, the path climbs up to Foel Goch.

Our next objective is the peak with the lyrical-sounding name of Moel Cynghorion (hill of the councillors), whose grassy summit is visible ahead beyond the dip of Bwlch Maesgwm. From Foel Goch, steep grassy slopes descend south-east alongside a wire fence to a stile at a junction of walls and fences at Bwlch Maesgwm. Ahead is an obvious path, which climbs up alongside another fence on the ridge to the wide

The Snowdon range reflected in Llyn Padarn.

The Nantlle hills seen from the slopes of Foel Gron.

Leaving the summit slopes of Snowdon for Llanberis. Moel Eilio in the distance.

Walkers heading towards Moel Cynghorion, with Moel Eilio in the background.

grassy summit of Moel Cynghorion, its high point at 674m/2211 feet from where you get an excellent view back along the scalloped cwms to Moel Eilio. But it is the scene south-east across Bwlch Cwm Brwynog to the cliffs of Clogwyn Du'r Arddu (the black cliff), backed by Snowdon's summit, which catches your attention; this is a sight to savour, and a good excuse for a rest.

Moel Cynghorion to Yr Wyddfa

Descending the lip of the precipitous slopes of Clogwyn Llechwedd Llo on the north-east flank of Moel Cynghorion, the path continues south-east down towards the little reservoir of Llyn Ffynnon-y-gwas, to arrive at Bwlch Cwm Brwynog. After the long descent of nearly 180m/600 feet, the grassy terrain is now replaced with the stony Snowdon Ranger Path just below the col. The constructed path zigzags up the southern flank of the main ridge sweeping up towards Snowdon itself.

Although you can ascend the Snowdon Ranger path, a much more exciting way is to detour left up the crest of the ridge from where you get breathtaking views down the great cliffs of Clogwyn Du'r Arddu, the finest crag in Wales and affectionately known

simply as 'Cloggy' to generations of rock climbers. To stand near the dark, brooding waters of Llyn Du'r Arddu, which lies in a hollow at the foot of the precipices, and gaze up at them, is to feel a sense of awe at their magnificent architecture. Numerous classic rock climbs weave their way up the steep vertical walls and overlapping slabs. Although only tantalizing views of the buttresses can be had from the summit ridge, non-climbers can sense the majesty of the place.

The angle eventually eases and you soon reach a marker stone by the railway line and broad path from Llanberis. The next larger marker stone, a short distance up the path, indicates the start of the descent route of the Miners' and Pig Tracks to the east. Snowdon's summit, with its café, train terminal and usual crowds – certainly in summer – is at a higher level up to the north-east. The summit of Yr Wyddfa (the tomb), at 1085m/3560 feet, is not a place for the walker who seeks solitude, but it does provide a marvellous panorama of mountain scenery and one that never fails to delight.

Yr Wyddfa to Llanberis

The return leg now involves either following the path alongside the railway line – difficult when icy – back to Llanberis, or the more attractive option of veering right at Clogwyn Station and descending a ridge towards the impressive cliff of Llechog. From Lechog's slabby summit you get excellent views west across Cwm Brwynog to Cloggy and the undulating ridge stretching from Moel Cynghorion to Moel Eilio, crossed earlier in the day.

Continuing down the grassy ridge top you cross the other Tryfan – from where you get a bird's-eye-view of Nant Peris – and finally Derlwyn, whose slopes lead gently down to join the main Llanberis Path just before it reaches the tarmac road descending into the town.

A snow-capped Snowdon rises beyond the cliffs of Clogwyn Du'r Arddu.

INFORMATION
Start/Finish: Llanberis.
Distance: 19.3km/12 miles.
Walking Time/total climb: 6–8 hours/ 1520m(5000 feet).
Grading: Very Difficult; a long walk over high mountain terrain with lots of ups and downs.
Maps: OS Explorer OL17.
Refreshments: Summit café and various cafes, including Pete's Eats, and pubs in Llanberis.
Transport: Buses from Bangor and Caernarfon; also regular Snowdon Sherpa buses which also provide a rail connection at Betws-y-Coed.

The Miners' Track from Pen-y-Pass.

The first stage of this fascinating and varied walk follows the Miners' Track from Pen-y-Pass, and is one of the most popular ways up Snowdon. Formerly used to bring copper ore from the mines in Cwm Dyli, this wide stony track, now well constructed and pitched in its steep upper section, passes through some superb mountain scenery.

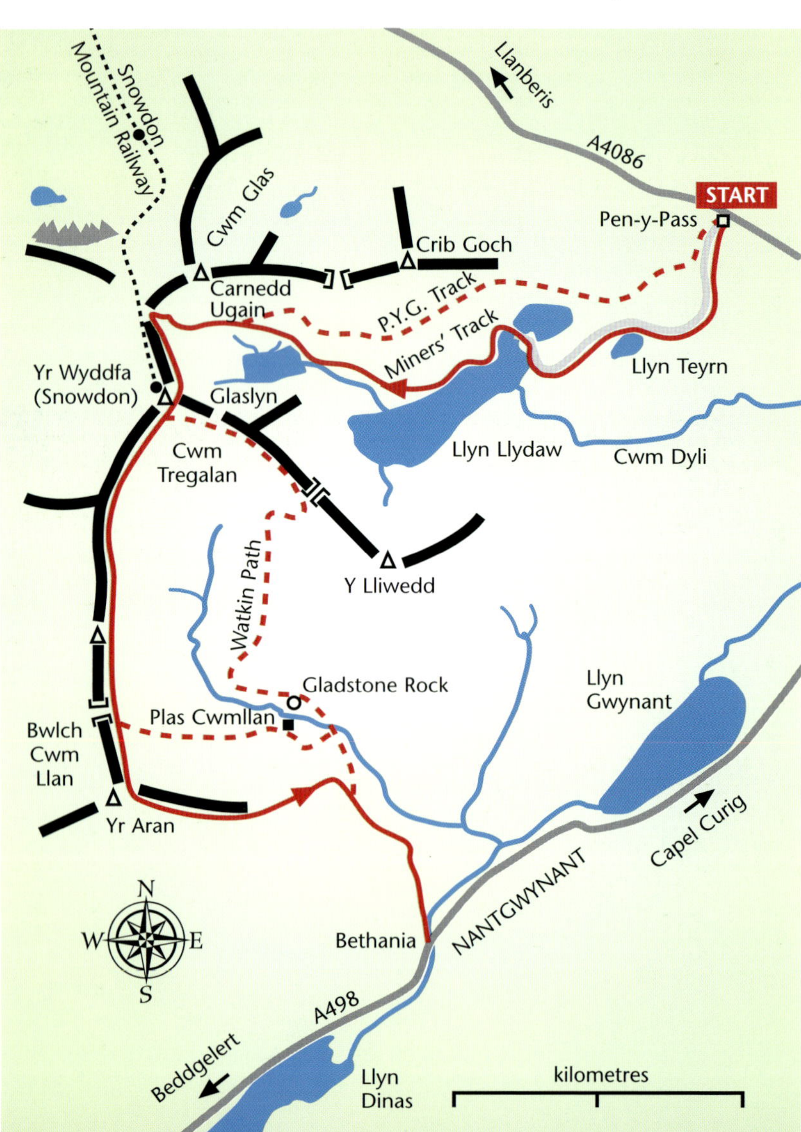

Although you could return by the same route, this outing involves either a descent of the Watkin Path to Pont Bethania in Nantgwynant, or the more challenging route of Snowdon's south ridge to the wedge-shaped peak of Yr Aran, whose east ridge leads down to meet the Watkin Path just above Bethania. The start and finish points of the walk are linked by the Snowdon Sherpa bus allowing a full traverse of Snowdon.

Pen-y-Pass to Yr Wyddfa

Pen-y-Pass, at the head of Llanberis Pass, has a large café, youth hostel and (expensive) car park, which fills up very quickly. The obvious broad Miners' Track leaves the lower car park and leads south round a broad shoulder overlooking the Gwynant valley. An alternative, and also popular route, though significantly rockier, is the P.Y.G. Track, which leaves the top right corner of the car park behind the café and traverses the southern slopes of Crib Goch. It passes below the cliffs of Crib y Ddysgl and above the waters of Glaslyn to eventually joining the Miners' Track in the upper stages of the ascent.

The Miners' Track passes the first of three lakes, Llyn Teyrn, just beyond which the reservoir of Llyn Llydaw comes into view, bridged by a causeway and backed by the graceful cone of Yr Wyddfa. Once across the causeway, the track passes some derelict copper mine buildings, site of a sorting and crushing mill, which was worked by a water wheel supplied by a leat from Glaslyn higher up the cwm. These buildings were part of the Britannia Copper Mine, which was opened in the late eighteenth century and worked until the First World War. Until the Pen-y-Pass road was opened early in the nineteenth century the ore used to be taken from the shore of Glaslyn over Bwlch Glas between Snowdon and Carnedd Ugain. Then horse-drawn sledges took the ore down to Snowdon Ranger where it was taken by horse-drawn carts to Caernarfon.

Beyond the derelict buildings the track climbs steeply up to the hidden upper lake of Glaslyn, a classic glacial feature 38m/126 feet deep, whose waters are sometimes a startling blue-green caused by dissolved copper salts from the underlying rocks. From the outflow of Glaslyn, a rocky spur sweeps up south towards Bwlch y Saethau, the dip between Lliwedd and Snowdon. This soaring, undulating ridge with its rough slabs, rocky ribs, grooves and ledges is Cribau (Y Gribin) and forms part of the rim of Cwm Glaslyn. The ridge provides an exhilarating and usually quiet approach to Snowdon.

Ahead now lies a steep climb up a constructed path leading to a junction with the P.Y.G. Track and then a rising traverse up some zigzags – a particularly dangerous slope when covered in snow and ice. The path tops out beside a large, leaning marker stone at Bwlch Glas, with the Snowdon Railway rack and pinion track just beyond.

The summit of Snowdon (Yr Wyddfa) at 1085m/3560 feet, with its nearby train terminus, café, crowds and associated noise, is now just a short distance away along the track to the south-east. The top provides a breathtaking panorama of mountain scenery and one that never fails to delight.

Lliwedd reflected in Llyn Teyrn.

The Snowdon range seen across Nantgwynant.

Approaching Gladstone Rock along the Watkin Path.

Snowdon and Cwm Tregalan seen from Nantgwynant.

Crib Goch overlooking Llyn Llydaw.

Approaching Llyn Llydaw along the Miners' Track.

Yr Wyddfa to Nantgwynant

Leaving behind the summit crowds, the walk now follows a path down the south ridge for a short distance to the Watkin Path junction, a justly popular descent route via Cwm Tregalan. A more exciting option though, and certainly less crowded, is to continue straight ahead along the narrow crest of Bwlch Main. The ridge contours around the head of Cwm Tregalan, down Clogwyn Du and over the minor top of Allt Maenderyn. From this fine ridge you can look south-east into the lower Cwm Llan down to the remains of derelict buildings scattered amongst the moraine slopes of quarried slate.

Beyond Allt Maenderyn, the ridge drops steeply to the quarry workings at Bwlch Cwm Llan. This was once a crossing point for the miners from the quarries in Cwm Llan to get back to their homes at Rhyd Ddu. If legs are weary and you want to miss out shapely Yr Aran looming ahead then you can descend east from the col down easy slopes to a broad terrace, which once carried a horse-drawn tramway, part of the now-derelict South Snowdon Slate Quarry.

From the broad terrace the path eventually joins the Watkin Path just south of the ruins of Plas Cwmllan – once the home of the quarry manager – and downstream from the Gladstone Rock. During the last war, this area was used as a training ground by commandos, and the walls of Plas Cwmllan are still pock-marked with bullet holes.

The Watkin Path was presented to the nation in 1892 by the Victorian railway magnate and Liberal MP, Sir Edward Watkin, and was officially opened by the then 84-year-old Prime Minister W.E. Gladstone. He addressed a crowd from a low rock and hymns were sung; an event commemorated by the inscribed tablet on the famous rock. By descending the lower section of the Watkin Path you soon reach Bethania in Nantgwynant.

However, if Yr Aran (the high ridge) is your objective, then a steep broken rocky face beyond the col has to be followed. The summit is finally reached via an airy scramble on a shaly cliff, or more easily, by a path which ascends diagonally up to join the south-east ridge a short distance below the summit. The effort is worth while, especially for the dramatic view back up the south ridge to the pyramidal summit of Snowdon overlooking the shattered upper slopes of Cwm Tregalan. To the west you get an excellent perspective of Moel Hebog, the Nantlle Hills and Mynydd Mawr.

Leaving the stunning views behind, the crest of the broadening south-east ridge is descended through the Snowdonia National Nature Reserve to join the lower reaches of the Watkin Path. The path winds its way down to the foot of a hillside covered in mature oaks and the ubiquitous rhododendrons at Pont Bethania and the peaceful confines of Nantgwynant.

Snowdon and the sunlit Cribau (Y Gribin) seen from the shore of Llyn Llydaw.

INFORMATION

Start/Finish: The car park at Pen-y-Pass GR: 647556 and finishes at Pont Bethania GR: 628507. Better to park in Nant Peris and take the Snowdon Sherpa bus to Pen-y-Pass. Start and finish linked by Snowdon Sherpa bus.

Distance: 13km/8 miles.

Walking Time/total climb: 6-8 hours/ 1100m (3560 feet).

Grading: Very Difficult; a high mountain walk on mainly good paths but involves some steep rocky ascents and descents.

Maps: OS Explorer OL17.

Refreshments: The summit café on Snowdon and Gorphwysfa café at Pen-y-Pass. Pubs and cafes in Llanberis, Beddgelert and Capel Curig.

Transport: Buses from Bangor and Caernarfon; also regular Snowdon Sherpa buses which provide a rail connection at Betws-y-Coed.

The final scramble to the summit of Yr Aran.

Traversing around the Crib Goch pinnacles.

The Snowdon Horseshoe is the crème de la crème of Snowdonia's walks, and under-standably so. Despite the erosion, polished rocks and crowds, few would disagree that this ever-popular ridge walk is still one of the best easy scrambling excursions in Britain. It is challenging, exposed, has breathtaking views and you need a head for heights especially when traversing the exposed Crib Goch pinnacles. Normally the horseshoe is not too technically difficult during the summer months – except when it is very windy – but under snow and ice it becomes a serious undertaking requiring experience, winter equipment and the knowledge of how to use it.

Starting from Pen-y-Pass, the circuit involves crossing the summits of Crib Goch, Carnedd (or Garnedd) Ugain (more often known as Crib y Ddysgl), Yr Wyddfa and the twin-topped Lliwedd. The circuit is best done anti-clockwise so that you ascend the main scrambling sections.

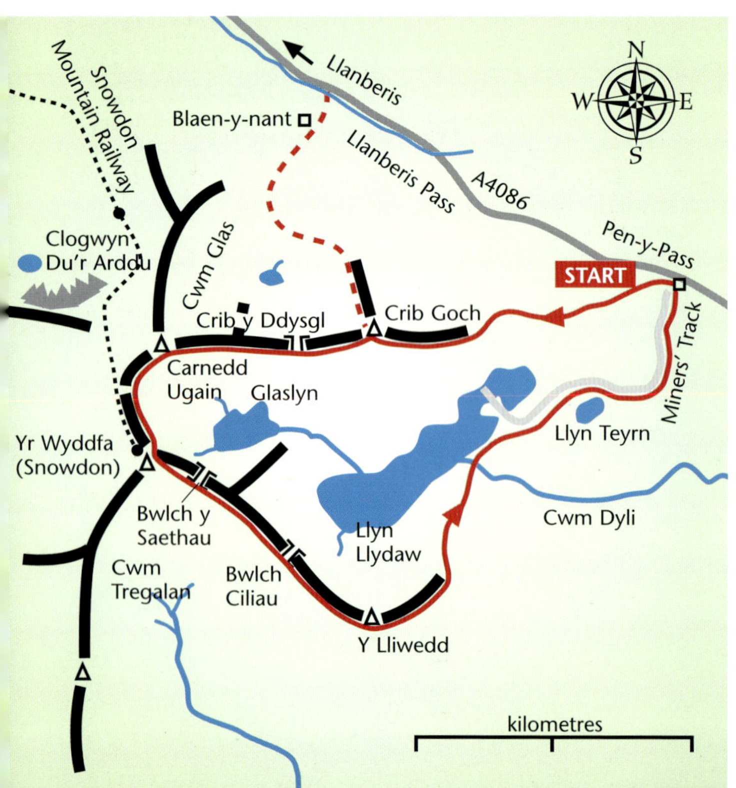

Pen-y-Pass to Yr Wyddfa

From the top right-hand corner of the car park at Pen-y-Pass a path heads towards Llanberis Pass and then swings left to climb up towards Crib Goch. This is the P.Y.G. Track and it gradually climbs diagonally across the hillside to the pass of Bwlch y Moch. Along this section you can look across to Lliwedd and the symmetrical cone of Snowdon.

At the pass, the P.Y.G. Track heads downhill to traverse the flank of Crib Goch, while our way is directly ahead up the steep East Ridge. There is a steep rocky part in the broad middle section involving some scrambling, above which the ridge narrows, ending with a few exposed moves up to the top of Crib Goch (red ridge) its high point at 923m/3028 feet, with the spectacular, narrow ridge and pinnacles clearly seen ahead. You also have excellent views left into the great, rocky hollow enclosed by the Snowdon Horseshoe while to the right is the ice-carved Cwm Glas and Llanberis Pass.

Cwm Glas provides a very good alternative approach to the summit of Crib Goch via its well-defined North Ridge. There is less scrambling than on Crib Goch's East Ridge and you will certainly meet fewer walkers. The North Ridge sweeps down into Llanberis Pass terminating abruptly at the impressive cliffs of Dinas Mot with its detached buttress of grey rock known as The Nose. Starting from the road near Blaen-y-nant, a footpath is followed steeply up into Cwm Glas Mawr, passing the left flank of the huge cliff of Cyrn Las via a zigzag path up scree slopes. By trending left you arrive at a red scree slope at the foot of the narrow section of Crib Goch's North Ridge. The ridge is easily followed until just below the summit, where an exposed rocky arête concentrates the mind for a few awkward moves.

The Snowdon Horseshoe at dawn seen across Llynnau Mymbyr.

Ascending Crib y Ddysgl backed by Snowdon.

Above left: *The Crib Goch pinnacles.*

Above right: *Crib Goch and Cwm Glas Mawr seen across the Llanberis Pass.*

Whichever option is chosen to reach the summit, walkers are still faced by a traverse along Crib Goch's narrow, exposed and almost horizontal arête and rocky pinnacles followed by an ascent of the pinnacled ridge up Crib y Ddysgl.

On calm days confident walkers may balance along the actual crest, others will use the crest as handholds with their feet on good, though polished, footholds on the left side, so avoiding the steep drop right into Cwm Uchaf. Ahead are the Crib Goch Pinnacles, which straddle the ridge and are turned on the left, but with care their tops can be safely crossed involving some scrambling in exposed situations. Beyond the pinnacles a small scree gully drops down to the flat Bwlch Coch.

Ahead is the long pleasant ridge of Crib y Ddysgl (ridge of the dish) which is always interesting but the scrambling is never really difficult up numerous rocky steps and a few knife-edge sections of broken rocks. Eventually the ridge levels off at the summit of Carnedd Ugain. During the ascent you can look back to the splintered crest of Crib Goch's pinnacles and across to the cliffs of Clogwyn y Garnedd, which form the craggy north-east face of Snowdon.

Despite Carnedd Ugain at 1065m/3494 feet being the second highest top in Wales, it suffers from its close proximity to Snowdon's summit, and is rarely ascended for its own sake. From the trig point a short descent lands you at Bwlch Glas from where the broad path follows the railway to the summit, at 1085m/3560 feet, the highest point of the mountain kingdom of Eryri. On a clear day you can look out from the roof of Wales and survey a marvellous panorama of mountain scenery; a fresh vision at every turn.

Crib Goch's north ridge is an alternative approach to the summit.

The Snowdon Horseshoe seen from the east.

Above: *A winter crossing of Lliwedd.*
Left: *Walkers silhouetted on Crib y Ddysgl.*

INFORMATION

Start/Finish: The car park at Pen-y-Pass GR: 647556. Better to park in Nant Peris and take the Snowdon Sherpa bus to Peny-y-Pass. Or park near the Pen-y-Gwryd hotel, and walk up the busy road to Pen-y-Pass.

Distance: 12km/7½ miles.

Walking Time/total climb: 6 to 8 hours/ 1000m (3300 feet).

Grading: Very Difficult; a high mountain walk on mainly well-defined paths but also involving some steep rocky ascents and descents, with some scrambling in exposed situations. A serious expedition under real winter conditions.

Maps: OS Explorer OL17.

Refreshments: The summit café on Snowdon and Gorphwysfa café at Pen-y-Pass. Cafes and pubs in Llanberis, Beddgelert and Capel Curig.

Transport: Buses from Bangor and Caernarfon; also regular Snowdon Sherpa buses which provide a rail connection at Betws-y-Coed.

Yr Wyddfa to Pen-y-Pass

Leaving the summit crowds behind, the horseshoe continues down Snowdon's steep south ridge where a rocky, twisting path weaves a way through numerous short outcrops soon joining the well-cairned Watkin Path. The path slants left down steep shale and shattered rock to the level ground at Bwlch y Saethau (the pass of the arrows). Here there are a couple of tiny lakes and a good view down to Glaslyn nestling below the shattered cliffs of Snowdon's north-east face.

According to Welsh legend this col is where King Arthur fought his final battle in the sixth century, when he and his knights faced Mordred and an army of Saxons. Arthur was fatally wounded by an arrow and was buried at the bwlch under a heap of stones. It is said his followers still sleep in a cave on the east face of Lliwedd awaiting a further call. However, at this stage images of battles and questions of its authenticity are far from most walkers' minds, for ahead lies the ascent of Lliwedd.

The climb starts after crossing undulating rocky terrain to the large cairn at Bwlch Ciliau and a major path junction; the obvious Watkin Path dipping to the right into Cwm Llan, and the worn path for Lliwedd (the hue) rising straight ahead. The climb up the north-west ridge to the first rocky summit is straightforward but by keeping to the very edge of the ridge some further scrambling can be had. The traverse over Lliwedd's two tops, the highest at 898m/2946 feet, gives a dramatic bird's-eye-view down the 300m/1000 feet north-facing cliffs to Llyn Llydaw and across to the crenellated ridge of Crib Goch.

Once across the rocky crest of Lliwedd, a stony path crosses over the little hump of Lliwedd Bach and then descends north-east towards the east end of Llyn Llydaw. From the lake, the Miners' Track gives a gentle stroll back to Pen-y-Pass, giving time for the mind to linger over the pleasure of a day spent 'nailing' the Snowdon Horseshoe.

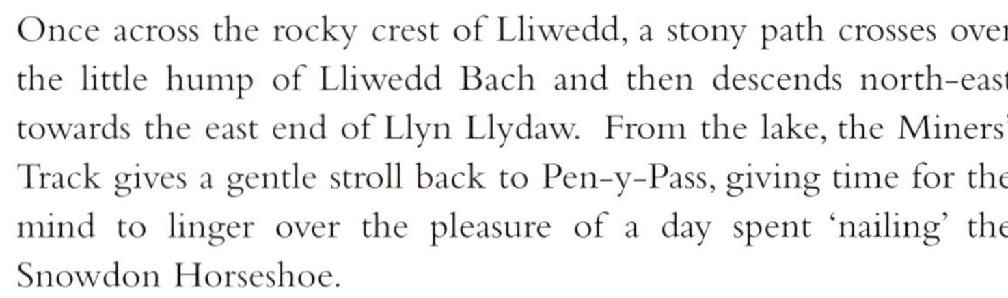

Starting the crossing of the Crib Goch pinnacles.

Above: *Lliwedd in its winter cloak.*

Above right: *Excellent easy scrambling up Crib y Ddysgl.*

Right: *Winter on the Snowdon Horseshoe.*

A foxglove growing among slate tips.

The craggy Craig Cwm Silyn.

4 THE NANTLLE (EIFIONYDD) HILLS

The small hills of Nantlle (often known as Eifionydd) lie to the south-west of the Snowdon range. The main group of these hills is situated to the south of the B4418 road linking Rhyd Ddu, Nantlle and Penygroes, and west of the A4085 Rhyd Ddu to Beddgelert road. Mynydd Mawr, often called the 'elephant mountain' because of its shape seen from the southern slopes of Snowdon, lies just to the north of the Rhyd Ddu to Nantlle road.

There are no majestic, soaring ridges here, nor the dramatic cwms of the Snowdon massif or the Glyderau. Here the valleys are softened by woodland, particularly around Beddgelert, with the Colwyn Valley forests and Aberglaslyn Pass. The modest height of these hills also means that walkers can spend more time really getting to know this quiet area. Being on the seaward side of Snowdonia, the views from the main summits of the Eifionydd hills are wonderful, especially of the coastline stretching from the Llyn Peninsula, with the conspicuous Yr Eifl hills, to Black Rock Sands and around to Harlech. There are also great views of the Snowdon range.

The Nantlle Ridge and the peaks to the north-west of Beddgelert collectively form the skyline of Cwm Pennant, one of Snowdonia's quietest and most beautiful valleys. A full traverse of the Nantlle Ridge is one of the great walks in the area, albeit on a different scale and character to the Snowdon Horseshoe. Although the Nantlle hills are mainly smooth and grassy, there are a few narrow ridges in places, which give some pleasant scrambling. Also an excellent half-day walk can be enjoyed by ascending Mynydd Mawr from Rhyd Ddu.

For many years the Nantlle Ridge and Mynydd Mawr suffered from access restrictions resulting in negotiation of access routes in the early 1980s. In recent years, and certainly with the implementation of the CROW Act, access to this excellent area is assured.

Moel Hebog dominates the village of Beddgelert and looks a real mountain whose wedge-shaped top is visible from miles around. The village is situated at the junction of the Colwyn and Glaslyn rivers, before the latter rushes through the wooded confines of Aberglaslyn Pass, eventually joining the sea at Tremadog. The village name means 'the grave of Gelert', a faithful hound who allegedly was mistakenly killed by a prince who assumed his baby had been killed by the dog, only to find the culprit was a wolf. Thought to be a story made up by the landlord of The Goat Hotel in the late nineteenth century, it certainly attracts sentimentalists to Beddgelert who flock to visit the gravestone.

Sadly the Nantlle area has not escaped the ravages of slate quarrying in the past and there are still numerous relics and spoil heaps at the head of Cwm Pennant and around Nantlle and Penygroes. Fortunately, Nature is now slowly reclaiming the landscape.

Transport to the Nantlle area is by bus from Caernarfon and Tremadog, Snowdon Sherpa buses in high season and the narrow-gauge Welsh Highland Railway, which now links Caernarfon with Rhyd Ddu. Bunkhouse accommodation and camping is also available at Rhyd Ddu. However, Beddgelert, with its campsite, B&Bs and hotels is the most popular centre for exploring these hills.

Above left: *Y Garn seen from the slopes of Mynydd Mawr.*

Above right: *Moel Hebog dominates the view across Llyn Gwynant.*

Remains of old slate quarries at the head of Cwm Pennant.

Despite the Nantlle hills being relatively small, this big dipper circular walk around part of the Cwm Pennant skyline is one of the best ridge walks in North Wales. Starting from Rhyd Ddu, here is a walk where you can escape the crowds, and it's also rich in history and industrial archaeology, relics of a bygone industrial age when miners toiled for copper and slate here.

Cwm Pennant lies at the heart of the hills of Eifionydd, and is one of the most delectable and isolated valleys in Snowdonia. Its head is enclosed to the north and west by the peaks of the Nantlle Ridge, and to the east by the high ridge of Moel Hebog. A narrow lane winds north into the valley from the A487 Porthmadog to Caernarfon road, crossing and re-crossing the peaceful Afon Dwyfor.

Many cultures have left their mark here and the area is dotted with signs of human activity dating back to prehistoric times, the most famous being the ruins of Iron and Bronze Age round and long huts on the southern flanks of Moel Hebog. Today Cwm Pennant contains a scattering of hill farms, some deserted, and the way of life is strongly dependent on sheep farming.

Rhyd Ddu to Cwm Pennant

The walk starts opposite the National Park car park near Rhyd Ddu, where a slated path crosses a marshy field then skirts round the cottage of Tan y Llyn. After crossing the left hand of two footbridges, the path leads to the Rhyd Ddu – Nantlle road. Turning immediately left through a gate, a path takes you towards the shapely Y Garn. The way is obvious and unrelentingly steep, but the widely-opening views back to the huge western flanks of Snowdon take your mind off the ascent. Eventually, grass yields to scree slopes up to the rocky top of Y Garn (the cairn) at 633m/2077 feet. From here you can look across the Nantlle Valley to Mynydd Mawr and the shattered cliffs and ridges of Craig y Bera.

From the summit of Y Garn, a drystone wall leads your eye up towards the wedge-shaped Mynydd Drws-y-coed (the mountain of the wooded gap) and on to Trum y Ddysgl (the ridge of the dish). The ascent of the slender, splintered crest of Clogwyn Marchnad, which leads to the summit of Mynydd Drws-y-coed, provides the trickiest part of the route. Exposed and rocky, the easy scramble is a delight, although all difficulties can be easily avoided. A narrow arête finally sweeps up to the grassy-topped Trum y Ddysgl (709m/2326 feet).

The walk continues over short-cropped turf down to a gentle col then up to the easily recognisable top of Mynydd Tal-y-mignedd (653m/2142 feet) complete with its chimney-like tower, which makes up for the general lack of cairns in this area. Constructed to celebrate Queen Victoria's Diamond Jubilee in 1897, this well-made obelisk is visible from most tops during the walk. From here you are supposed to be able to see the castles of Caernarfon, Harlech and Criccieth.

Above: *Looking north-east along the Nantlle Ridge from Craig Cwm Silyn.*

Below left: *Mynydd Drws-y-coed seen from the slopes of Y Garn.*

Below right: *A steep, narrow ridge leads up to the summit of Mynydd Drws-y-coed.*

Above left: *Y Garn (left) and Mynydd Mawr.*

Above right: *Renovated water wheel in Cwm Ciprwth.*

From the summit a ridge dips south-west to the little used pass of Bwlch Dros-bern, once a popular route linking the Nantlle and Pennant valleys. A stiff climb beyond the pass leads up the rocky north-east ridge of Craig Cwm Silyn (the rock of Silyn's valley), to the summit cairn at 734m/2408 feet. A steep rocky bit can be avoided by taking the path to the right of Craig Pennant, rejoining the ridge above the tricky section. The great attraction of Craig Cwm Silyn is the fine sculptured amphitheatre on its northern flanks containing two heart-shaped lakes.

From the western end of the cliffs, you now bear south-west across an undulating plateau to reach Garnedd Goch (red cairn), with its OS trig point at 700m/2297 feet. Continuing alongside a wall, the ridge gradually loses height down bouldery slopes to Bwlch Cwmdulyn at the head of Cwm Ciprwth. A faint path now descends south-east across heather-clad slopes into Cwm Ciprwth. The path drops alongside a stream to a fascinating restored cast-iron water wheel, a relic of the nearby Gilfach copper-mine. A narrow bridge across the stream gives access to the huge black wheel used to pump water from the nearby shafts. During the descent into this peaceful cwm you are accompanied by breathtaking views across the verdant Cwm Pennant to Moel Hebog.

Cwm Pennant to Rhyd Ddu

Continuing alongside the stream, passing some sheepfolds, you then head left along an old mine path down through conservation woodland towards the road in the

INFORMATION

Start/Finish: Car park at Rhyd Ddu, GR: 569529.

Distance: 24km/15 miles.

Walking Time/total climb: 7 hours/ 1075m (3526 feet).

Grading: Difficult; a long and strenuous route on mainly good paths but with several rocky sections (difficulties can be avoided).

Maps: OS Explorer OL17.

Refreshments: Cwellyn Arms, Rhyd Ddu.

Transport: Served by buses from Caernarfon and Tremadog, and Snowdon Sherpa buses in high season. Train from Caernarfon to Rhyd Ddu.

valley bottom. At the foot of a wooded gully, a waymarked path crosses the wooded hillside right to Gilfach Farm from where a track leads left to join the valley road. Heading right here, the road is followed towards our next objective, Cwrt Isaf farm.

After about 500m/550 yards a stile is reached on the left by a cattle grid. Once over the stile, a field is crossed to a series of stepping-stones over the Afon Dwyfor. The path continues through fields, crosses a metalled lane – an alternative approach if the river is in spate – and then more fields to join a grassy lane, which bears left to the farm of Cwrt Isaf. A waymarked path leads past a barn, then climbs up the hillside on the left bank of the Afon Cwm-llefrith towards the obvious dip on the skyline linking Moel Hebog and Moel yr Ogof.

The path soon reaches the former railway track from the old slate quarries at the head of the valley. Our way is now left along the grassy track-bed eventually passing some buildings near the base of an incline, which climbs up through old mine workings. After passing along the northern shore of a small lake, an often ill-defined path climbs up through the remains of the old Prince of Wales Slate Quarry. Here, dark purple waste tips, deep, silent derelict quarries and old slate buildings are all lasting testaments to a harsh way of life the miners experienced. The quarry was once linked by a railway which can be traced to Porthmadog.

Continuing up the path you arrive at Bwlch-y-Ddwy-elor (the pass of the two biers), an old corpse road connecting Cwm Pennant with Rhyd Ddu in the days before there was a church in Cwm Pennant. Beyond the col the Beddgelert Forest is entered, where paths and tracks can be followed north-east down through a conifer plantation. Once clear of the forest, a bridleway traverses the lower grassy slopes of Cwm Marchnad back towards Rhyd Ddu.

Superb walking along the Nantlle Ridge.

Descending the east ridge of Mynydd Tal-y-mignedd on the Nantlle Ridge.

The shapely peak of Moel Hebog seen across Llyn Gwynant.

Moel Hebog (the hill of the hawk) is a remote, wedge-shaped hill standing high above the village of Beddgelert. Seen from Llyn Dinas in the Vale of Gwynant, the peak looks majestic and is an obvious attraction to walkers. This described walk up Moel Hebog from Beddgelert, via Cwm Cloch, is very steep and involves some easy scrambling up broken rocks and scree, but the effort is worthwhile because its isolated position provides a magnificent viewpoint.

The walk then continues along the undulating ridge over the satellite peaks of Moel yr Ogof and Moel Lefn, before returning to Beddgelert by paths and tracks through forest, which cloaks the eastern flanks of the range. You can also seek out a cave on Moel yr Ogof linked with Owain Glyndwr, leader of the last Welsh rebellion against the English.

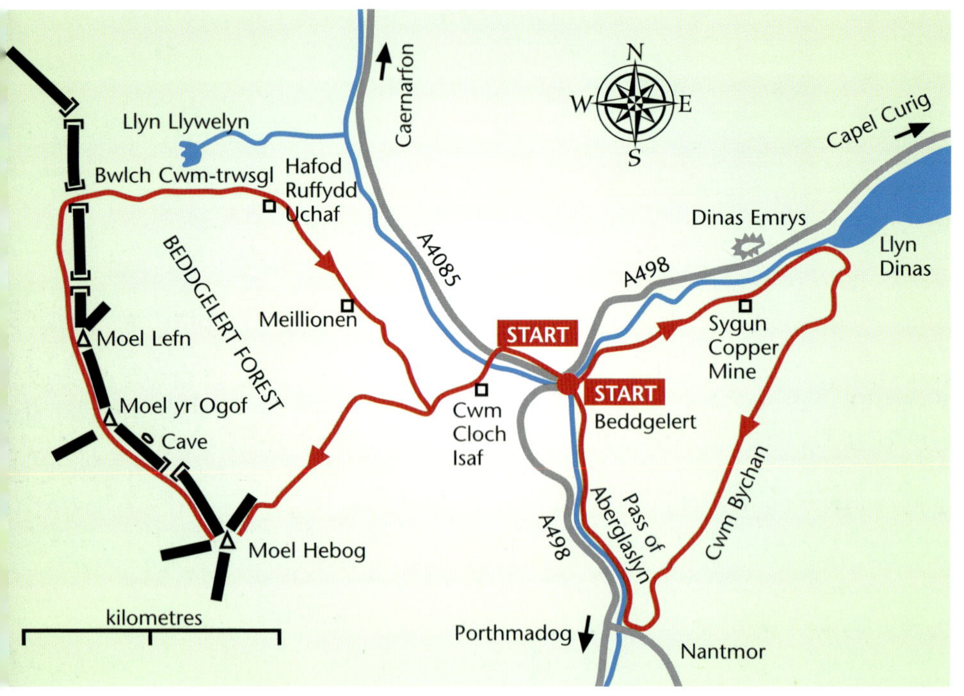

Beddgelert to Moel Hebog

The walk starts on the A4085 Beddgelert to Caernarfon road about 500m/550 yards from the road junction in the centre of the village. Here, a leafy lane leads left across a bridge to Cwm Cloch Isaf Farm. Immediately after a barn, a waymarked path crosses usually wet ground to reach the base of Hebog's broad, north-eastern ridge. The grassy path eventually leads up to rockier ground and the top of Diffwys, a prominent broken cliff clearly seen from Beddgelert. When the angle eases it's only a short distance over scree and windswept turf to the trig-point on the summit dome of Moel Hebog (782 m/2565 feet).

Moel Hebog to Beddgelert

Leaving Moel Hebog, a steep grassy descent lands you at Bwlch Meillionen, a damp mossy col overlooked by the jumbled rocks of Moel yr Ogof, which are tackled up an obvious gully between steep rock walls. Moel yr Ogof (the hill of the cave) is linked to Owain Glyndwr, the Welsh leader who once supposedly sheltered from his enemies for six months in a cave under the eastern lip of the summit. By making a slight detour you can seek out this exposed, horizontal slot high above the wooded slopes of Beddgelert Forest.

A grassy ridge now leads over Moel yr Ogof and onwards to Moel Lefn overlooking the upper reaches of Cwm Pennant. Continuing north over the ridged summit a convoluted descent through an area of broken crags and bogs leads down to Bwlch Cwm-trwsgl. Turning right here, a stile gives access into Beddgelert Forest. A combination of waymarked paths and tracks descend east through the forest to meet a bridleway just beyond Hafod Ruffydd Uchaf. The bridleway is followed south-east through woodland and grassland via Meillionen, just west of the Forestry Commission campsite (GR: 577491). Eventually the bridleway reaches Cwm Cloch Isaf, passed earlier at the start of the walk.

From the farm, a narrow lane now leads down to the main road, which is followed right, back to Beddgelert accompanied by fine views of Moel Hebog.

Looking north from the summit of Moel Hebog.

Below left: *Steep slopes lead down towards Moel yr Ogof.*

Below right: *The cliffs of Moel yr Ogof contain a cave once used by Owain Glyndwr.*

Approaching the summit of Moel Hebog.

WALK 11a CWM BYCHAN AND THE PASS OF ABERGLASLYN

If the high tops are out of condition then an interesting low-level walk can be had exploring Cwm Bychan and the remains of the Sygun Copper Mine in the Gwynant valley. Starting from the bridge in Beddgelert, a path on the far side of the River Glaslyn is followed north-east to join a road which leads to the old Sygun copper mine. First opened in the late eighteenth century and finally abandoned in 1903, the mine is now a museum and popular tourist attraction.

On the other side of the valley from here is the prominent tree-shrouded mound of Dinas Emrys. Traditionally this is thought to have been the site of the fortress of Vortigern, the Dark Age ruler who let Saxon mercenary fighters into the country and was supposedly responsible in part for their later invasions. When the Saxons were driven west, legend has it that Vortigern chose this defensive location as a royal retreat. Archaeological excavations in the 1950s revealed that Dinas Emrys was occupied in the late Roman period. The most conspicuous ruin currently on the hill is the base of a rectangular tower, thought to have been built by the Welsh in the twelfth century.

After crossing the road for the mine workings, a path continues to the end of Llyn Dinas from where a steep zigzagging path leads up right to a prominent rocky outcrop at Bwlch y Sygyn; here you have fine views of the Snowdon range. Beyond the pass, a path leads down through Cwm Bychan, passing several old spoil heaps and rusting remains of an aerial ropeway which once carried buckets of ore down to a dressing plant near the bottom of the cwm.

If you had been on these hills in 1958 you would have seen the area transformed into the bleak landscape of war-torn China complete with village. It was the set for the film *The Inn of the Sixth Happiness*, which starred Ingrid Bergman. In the nearby Nantmor Valley there were even paddy fields and a section of a mock Great Wall of China. This must have been a surreal sight for unsuspecting walkers.

You now descend through fine woodland to Pont Aberglaslyn, from where a fisherman's riverside path can be followed along the eastern bank of the Afon Glaslyn through the beautiful tree-clad Aberglaslyn Pass. After some exciting boulder-hopping, negotiation of some awkward steps and wooden bridges, a good track is joined beyond some closed-off railway tunnels. The tunnels were part of the Welsh Highland Railway linking Caernarfon with Porthmadog. Although the line closed in 1937, there are plans to reopen this section and link it via Beddgelert to the recently-renovated Caernarfon to Rhyd Ddu line.

If the river is in spate then you can walk alongside the road back to Beddgelert. Sentimentalists can visit Gelert's Grave before strolling into Beddgelert.

Above: *Crossing the pass just north of Moel Lefn.*

Above right: *Aberglaslyn Pass.*

Right: *The sun sets beyond Moel Hebog.*

Cnicht seen across Cwm Croesor.

Derelict buildings at the disused Rhosydd Quarry.

5 THE MOELWYN HILLS

The Moelwyn hills (or Y Moelwynion) lie in an area of high ground bounded by the road from Betws-y-Coed to the Pen-y-Gwryd Hotel; the beautiful wooded valley of Nantgwynant; the lush vales of Glaslyn and Ffestiniog, and the A470 road which winds its way over the Crimea Pass alongside the Afon Lledr to Betws-y-Coed.

The main peaks of the range are shapely Moel Siabod, overlooking Capel Curig, the pointed Cnicht above Croesor, and the twin peaks of Moelwyn Bach and Moelwyn Mawr near Blaenau Ffestiniog. Situated between these main summits is a wild land-scape of convoluted rocky knolls and hollows, where you find more small lakes than in any other part of Snowdonia.

Numerous popular walks are to be found around and up the main peaks and there is also an excellent long outing taking in the neglected wild area of heather moorland and lakes extending from Moel Siabod's west ridge over Moel Meirch to Llyn Edno, then out along Ysgafell Wen's ridge to Cnicht and down to Croesor.

On the eastern flanks of the Moelwynion are the dammed Llyn Stwlan, Tanygrisiau hydroelectric power station and huge slate quarries and slate tips overlooking Blaenau Ffestiniog. On damp, cloudy days these tips and quarries impart a grim and sombre appearance to the surrounding area. Unlike the slate quarries at Llanberis and Bethesda, here the slate has been mined, with the largest site being the Oakley Quarry, which extended about 180m/600 feet under the town. When the hills are out of condition then a visit to the still working Llechwedd Quarry with its Slate Caverns tourist attraction is worthwhile. The area is also famous for its narrow gauge Ffestiniog Railway, which connects Blaenau Ffestiniog with Porthmadog, and thus the Conwy line with the Cambrian Coast.

If you want a closer look at some of the relics left behind from the slate quarrying industry, then a walk up an old quarry road above the small village of Tanygrisiau, to

the west of Blaenau Ffestiniog, will repay the effort. The track leads into Cwm Orthin and up to the Rhosydd Slate Quarry ruins at a high pass between Cnicht and Moelwyn Mawr. On the walk you can seek out an old chapel, a nineteenth century ghost town with relics of the workers' barracks, slate tips, mine entrances, inclines and old buildings where the slate was sliced up using water-powered saws.

The best centres for exploring the Moelwynion are Capel Curig and Beddgelert with their good bus links and wide range of accommodation in hotels, B&Bs, youth hostels and camp sites.

<h1>WALK 12   MOEL SIABOD FROM PONT CYFYNG</h1>

There are several routes up Moel Siabod, some easier than others, but this walk, starting from Pont Cyfyng on the A5 just south-east of Capel Curig, is arguably the best. This exhilarating approach includes an ascent of the Daear Ddu ridge above Llyn y Foel to the summit, returning by Moel Siabod's long and craggy north-east ridge. This is one of the best ridge walks in the area.

Few travellers heading from Betws-y-Coed along the road towards Capel Curig can fail to be impressed by the striking outline of the aloof Moel Siabod, sweeping up above woodlands on the left. With Moel Siabod commanding such an isolated position from the surrounding hills you are rewarded by fine views from its summit. Its rocky top, overlooking serrated ridges and precipitous buttresses, provides one of the finest viewpoints for the Snowdonia massif, which is revealed in all its glory.

Pont Cyfyng to Moel Siabod

From a lay-by at Pont Cyfyng you can peer over a wall down to the fast flowing waters of the Afon Llugwy. The river rushes through Capel Curig before passing under the nearby bridge where it plunges over the Cyfyng Falls; a fine sight when in spate.

Just after crossing the road bridge above the falls, the second of two footpath signs in about 100m/110 yards, points the way right up a steep track past Rhos Farm. Continuing along the track a fork is reached, the left branch leading to an old slate quarry, the right branch continuing across a bleak moor towards Moel Siabod's north-east ridge which rises directly ahead.

After reaching a pair of ladder stiles, the left one is crossed and the track followed past a small lake and then further on a flooded quarry hole, a reminder of how important slate quarrying and mining were to this part of Snowdonia. The track now swings south-west over a small rise and enters the glacial carved Cwm Foel, with Llyn y Foel cupped in a hollow beneath Moel Siabod's massive broken crags.

By following a path across the marshy hollow to the right of the lake you arrive at the foot of the obvious ridge of Daear Ddu, its broken cliff forming the back wall of the cwm. From the bottom of the ridge there is a splendid view south of the extensive moorlands and forests of the Lledr valley. You can also pick out the ruins of the prominent thirteenth century Dolwyddelan Castle, perched on the edge of a rocky crag in a commanding position above the Afon Lledr.

Llyn y Foel backed by the Daear Ddu ridge.

*A view across Capel Curig from
the slopes of Moel Siabod.*

Above left: *Walkers approaching Moel Siabod from the north.*

Above right: *Descending Moel Siabod's north-east ridge.*

INFORMATION
Start/Finish: The lay-by beside the A5 at Pont Cyfyng. GR: 731571.
Distance: 10.5km/6½ miles.
Walking Time/total climb: 5 hours/750m (2450 feet).
Grading: Moderate; mainly good paths along rocky ridges and involves some easy scrambling. The rocks become slippery when wet.
Maps: OS Explorer OL17.
Refreshments: Cafes and pubs at Capel Curig.
Transport: Served by buses between Betws-y-Coed and Bethesda.

Opposite page: *The summit of Moel Siabod peeps over woods near Capel Curig.*

A good path now leads up the Daear Ddu ridge, which veers right in its upper section. Here you can tease out numerous interesting scrambling problems on the rocky ridge, although most difficulties can be avoided. As you approach the summit of Moel Siabod (barren hill) you have a stunning view on the right into the depths of Cwm Foel. Soon the craggy ridge ends and you arrive at the stony plateau and summit trig point of Moel Siabod at 872m/2860 feet.

Moel Siabod to Pont Cyfyng

First time visitors here are often surprised to find that this attractive symmetrical peak seen from Capel Curig is really the end of a long ridge which sweeps south-west to Cnicht, yet another shapely peak, especially when viewed from the south, is in reality simply the other end of the ridge.

The views from the summit of Moel Siabod are superb and on a clear day you can savour the panoramic views of the main peaks in the National Park, but it is the ones to the west across Nantgwynant, which will grab your attention. Nowhere else do you get such a good view of the magnificent Snowdon Horseshoe.

The descent route now lies north-east down Moel Siabod's long summit ridge, crossing the numerous craggy rocks that straddle the crest, or more easily, keeping just below the crest on the left along a clear footpath. From the ridge you have a bird's-eye-view right down Cwm Foel to Llyn y Foel, while to the left, the Glyderau stretch across the skyline. Eventually you reach the ladder stiles and the approach route back to the start.

Descending north from Moelwyn Mawr towards Moelwyn Bach.

CNICHT, MOELWYN MAWR AND MOELWYN BACH FROM CROESOR

Starting from the tiny village of Croesor, high above the meadows of Traeth Mawr, this excellent outing crosses the rocky and shapely Cnicht and the pair of Moelwyn hills – Moelwyn Mawr and Moelwyn Bach. A feature of the walk is the section through an assortment of derelict slate quarrying and mine workings. This legacy of decay still has an impact on the landscape adding a strange beauty to the peace which has now returned to these hills. The industrial remains scattered around the hills are a very important part of the heritage of North Wales and, as such, add an extra dimension to this walk.

The shapeliest and certainly the best-known hill ascended along the walk is Cnicht, whose mountain-like profile belies its modest height of just 689m/2260 feet. Often called the Welsh Matterhorn, the hill's name is thought to be English; Cnicht being derived from *cnight,* an Old English word for a knight's helmet.

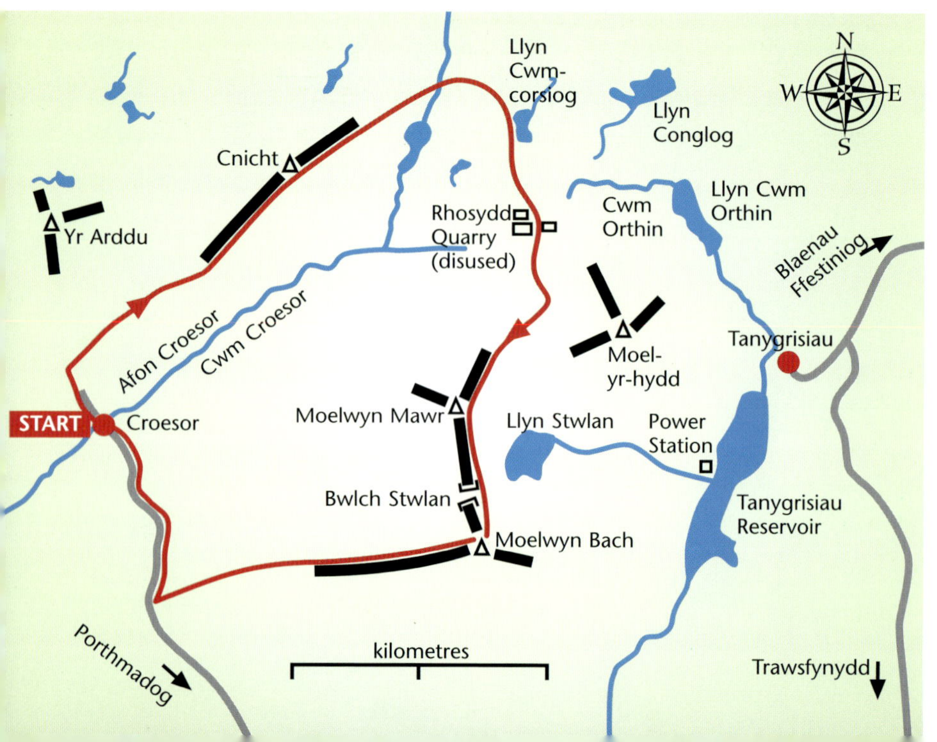

Croesor to Moelwyn Mawr

The small hamlet of Croesor is situated in a picturesque valley and is approached by a narrow hill road from the A4085 Beddgelert to Penrhyndeudraeth road. The hamlet is associated with the slate industry, which has formed such an integral part of the history and heritage of this region.

From the riverside car park at Croesor, a steep, narrow road climbs north-west out of the village past a chapel, to eventually join a rocky track beyond a gate and stile. The track climbs steeply up through woodland, and as it levels out, a waymarked path forks right leading to the

Cnicht seen across Cwm Croesor.

Looking down Cnicht's long south-west ridge.

main south-west ridge of Cnicht. This is a long steep ridge with some pleasant scrambling on a rocky tower just below the summit.

Cnicht's summit lies at the end of a long, undulating ridge and its great appeal is the breathtaking vista, which gradually unfolds as height is gained. On a clear day the panorama extends from the Snowdon group to the Nantlle hills, the Tremadog Estuary and the Harlech Dome backed by the distant Cadair Idris range.   Nearer at hand, across the glacial U-shaped valley of Cwm Croesor, sits the round-shouldered bulk of Moelwyn Mawr.

The final slopes leading to the summit of Cnicht.

Continuing north-east along Cnicht's ridge a secondary summit is crossed before veering right down to a marshy col above Cwm-y-foel. A meandering path, often wet, leads round to Llyn Cwm-corsiog and down to the disused slate mine ruins and derelict buildings at Bwlch y Rhosydd. The col is really a broad plateau hemmed in by surrounding hills and is a playground for industrial archaeologists. In dull weather this once thriving slate mining area, can be a very melancholic place, its decaying ruins a reminder of the harsh conditions that the slate workers had to endure to earn a mere pittance.

The surrounding hillsides once echoed to the sounds of drilling, sawing and splitting slate, the final products being transported down the great Rhosydd Quarry ramp into Cwm Croesor, then by tramway to Porthmadog for export all around the world. Abandoned in the 1920s, the decaying ruins of crumbling slate terraced houses now offer some shelter in bad weather and provide a good place for a spot of lunch. Although planning permission was granted in the 1990s to re-open this disused slate quarry, it seems unlikely that it will ever open again.

Alongside a stream at the entrance to an old mine adit, an obvious incline leads south up the hillside alongside a huge waste slate tip. The broken pieces of slate underfoot produce a surreal tinkling sound as you head up the incline, which leads in easy stages to grassy slopes and the obvious northern spur of Moelwyn Mawr. As height is gained the hillside becomes steeper especially just below the summit which overlooks the dam of Llyn Stwlan. As can be expected, you have superb views from Moelwyn Mawr (the big white hill), at 770m/2526 feet the high point of the walk. To the west the sea dominates the scene but inland you can pick out most of the major hills of Snowdonia and mid-Wales.

Crossing Cnicht's long summit ridge.

Moelwyn Mawr to Croesor

A ridge linking Moelwyn Mawr to Moelwyn Bach (little white
hill) starts innocently enough on smooth grass but then the path
suddenly drops steeply over some rocky steps before climbing over
the small craggy top of Craigysgafn. Crossing this section the view
is dominated by the rugged profile of Moelwyn Bach, while down
to the left nestles Llyn Stwlan, the upper dam of the Tanygrisiau
hydroelectric power station with its pumped storage system.

Continuing down a steep rocky ridge you arrive at the grassy
col of Bwlch Stwlan, above which looms the inaccesible-looking
Moelwyn Bach. The black craggy nose, blocking a view of the
actual summit, looks forbidding from here and seems to overhang
the screes just beyond the col. The steep rocks ahead are avoided
by a path, which ascends the scree-covered northern slopes of
Moelwyn Bach, up to the left, eventually veering right over a
number of small outcrops to the flat summit at 710m/2329
feet. Moelwyn Bach is guarded on three sides by rugged crags,
the fourth being the long, smooth and grassy west ridge. As from
its neighbour, Moelwyn Mawr, you have another fine outlook
from here.

After spending most of the day in a rocky environment, the
leisurely descent of the grassy western spur of Moelwyn Bach will
come as a welcome change. The scene of the late afternoon sun
reflected off the Glaslyn Estuary and Tremadog Bay shows yet
another facet of this ever-changing land of slate. After about
2km/1¼ miles along the ridge, you aim to the left of a small wood
to join a track, which passes through fields. Once a minor road is
reached it is then just an easy amble right, back to Croesor.

Ascending the east ridge of Moelwyn Mawr high above Stwlan Dam.

Slate fences line up like tombstones at the disused Rhosydd slate quarry.

The summit of Arenig Fawr.

Looking east from the Aran range.

6 THE BERWYN, ARENIG, ARAN AND DYFI HILLS

On the eastern flank of Snowdonia National Park is a broad undulating ridge stretching from Ruthin and the Clwydian hills in the north-east, to Machynlleth and the Taran range in the south-west. The individual groups of hills along this wide ridge, some of which are just outside the National Park, include the Clwydian and Llangollen hills, the Berwyn, the Hirnant hills, the Aran, the Arenig off to the west of Bala, the Dyffi hills and the Taran range to the south of Cadair Idris.

The Berwyn (or Y Berwynion – the snow-dusted peaks), situated just outside the National Park, consist of a broad ridge of scalloped peaks on the edge of a vast rolling area of spacious heather moorland offering discerning walkers a rare feeling of solitude. This vast mosaic of hills stretch as far as the eye can see as the moors decline east towards the Shropshire Plain and the Long Mynd, while to the north are the Denbigh Moors and the lonely Clwydian hills beyond Llangollen.

Many walkers driving along the A5 from Llangollen to Corwen – passing through Owain Glyndwr country – are so keen to reach the bigger hills of Snowdon, the Glyderau and Carneddau, that they barely give these rounded, rather dull-looking, heather-covered hills little more than a passing glance. For those walkers prepared to make a slight detour from the A5, and drive south from Corwen to Llandrillo, then their effort will be rewarded by a fine trek over five tops rising over 610m/2000 feet on a ridge stretching from Moel Fferna in the north to Milltir Gerrig in the south. Cadair Bronwen, Cadair Berwyn and Moel Sych form the heart of the range. For many visitors to the Berwyn, the highlight is Pistyll Rhaeadr, one of the highest waterfalls in Wales, and once described as one of the 'Seven Wonders of Wales'.

The Arenig (or Y Arenig – the upland) rise above a vast wild area of bogs and trackless, heather moorland known as the Migneint, either side of the A4212 road linking Bala with Trawsfynydd. Arenig Fawr, the highest and finest peak of the range, has five long ridges radiating out from its top, and lies to the south opposite the smaller Arenig Fach, the two being separated by a road, river and disused railway track. As you climb out of Bala towards the reservoir of Llyn Celyn, it is the craggy east face of Arenig Fawr which dominates the view across the lake.

By comparison, Arenig Fach, which overlooks the Migneint to the west and the hidden Llyn Arenig Fach to the east, looks deceptively dull, but if an ascent of Arenig Fach is combined with a crossing of the Migneint, you can experience one of the loneliest wilderness landscapes in Snowdonia. The name of the Migneint is derived from 'Mignen', which means a morass, and despite the area of bog and heather moorland being no respecter of dry feet, there is something very appealing about the place.

To the north of Llyn Celyn is another broad area of heather moorland usually known as the Eastern Migneint, with the rounded summit of Carnedd y Filiast (cairn of the greyhound bitch) being the dominant hill, which is linked to Arenig Fach by a grassy ridge. Again, apart from sheep, you will meet few other walkers as you wander along this broad moorland range, which deserves to be better known.

Llyn Arenig Fawr.

The Dyfi hills.

Sunset over Llyn Tegid (Bala Lake).

The limestone escarpments overlooking Llangollen.

The Aran range seen from the east.

The Aran (or Yr Aran – the heights) are a compact group of hills along a narrow ridge stretching for 15km/9 miles south from Llanuwchllyn on the southern shore of Llyn Tegid (or Bala Lake), to Dinis Mawddwy. Situated in the centre is Aran Fawddwy, which at 905m/2969 feet is only 31 feet short of being included as one of the fourteen '3000 footers' of the Snowdon, Glyderau and Carneddau ranges, making it the highest point in Wales south of them.

The western slopes of the range are gentle and grassy and in parts cloaked in forest, while seen from the north-east along the hill road from Llanuwchllyn to Dinis Mawddwy, you get a very contrasting view where almost the entire range appears to be craggy. At its southern end the ridge divides into two arms enclosing the impressive Cwm Cywarch, with its fine cirque of steep buttresses separated by deep gullies.

The Aran hills have been at the centre of the longest access dispute in Snowdonia. Practically all of this land up to the summit ridge is privately owned and managed by the Aran Society. Over recent years a permitted path along the summit ridge has allowed walkers to access the ridge, either from Dinas Mawddwy or Llanuwchllyn. Despite these restrictions the Aran ridge has been very popular with walkers. Improved access should be guaranteed after the implementation of the CROW Act.

To the west of Dinis Mawddwy stretching towards Dolgellau are the gentle grassy summits of the Dyfi (Dovey) hills, which overlook the vast area of the Dyfi Forest to the south. These hills are for walkers seeking solitude and wanting to escape from the crowds.

The local towns of Llangollen, Bala and Dolgellau, with their good bus links, B&Bs, hotels, hostels and campsites are ideal centres for exploring these hills.

Above: *A view west from the Aran ridge.*

Left: *The isolated dwelling of Cefngarw in the heart of the Migneint.*

Below: *Autumn reflections on Llyn Tegid (Bala Lake).*

WALK 14 PISTYLL RHAEADR AND THE BERWYN HILLS

The highlight of this splendid circular walk across the Berwyn hills is a view of the spectacular Pistyll Rhaeadr (the spout waterfall). The falls dominate the head of the narrow wooded valley to the north-west of the village of Llanrhaeadr-ym-Mochnant (the waterfall village). The famed cascade plunges for over 61m/200 feet from the escarpment of Craig y Mwn (crag of the buzzard) in a raging torrent of spray to give one of Wales' highest falls. This is a beautiful spot, especially so in autumn when the trees, which cling to the mossy sides of the rocky gorge through which the falls tumble, are clothed in flaming yellows and browns.

Many famous people have visited this spot including Dr Johnson, who, in the 1770s, described it simply as 'Very high and in rainy weather very copious', a lack-lustre description indeed. It needed George Borrow, the stalwart traveller who journeyed through Wales in 1854, to really capture the atmosphere of the place. In his *Wild Wales* he romantically described Pistyll Rhaeadr as being like 'an immense skein of silk agitated and disturbed by tempestuous blasts' or 'a profusion of long silvery threads or hairs'.

Although the Berwyn might lack the ruggedness of the western hills of Snowdonia, they should not be underestimated. It is a deceptively gentle area of rolling, heathery moorland but in wild weather it can be an inhospitable place. Henry II's army found this out in 1164 when they were forced back at the Berwyn when severe conditions prevented them from attacking the Welsh near Corwen.

Pistyll Rhaeadr to Moel Sych

Just to the right of Pistyll Rhaeadr, which is easily reached from the car park, a waymarked path leads up through a small wood. Beyond

the trees the path forks: the right branch leads to a lane which descends to a stream and then heads north up the picturesque narrow valley above the Nant y Llyn to its lake source, Llyn Lluncaws; the left branch – our way – zigzags steeply up towards the top of Pistyll Rhaeadr.

Eventually the path enters a shallow valley through which the Afon Dysgynfa flows over a series of cataracts hidden among the trees, before tumbling spectacularly over the crag edge. A marker post points the way to an exposed view from the top of the falls, although it's not as good as that from the foot of the cascades. The path now leads north-west into the heart of the moorland landscape.

Crossing the lower slopes of Moel Sych.

Heading into the valley beyond Pistyll Rhaeadr.

Looking north from Cadair Berwyn.

The rocky summit of Cadair Berwyn overlooking Llyn Lluncaws.

About 1km/2/3 mile up the valley, the Afon Disgynfa is joined by the Nant Y Cerig-duon, which flows down the slopes on the right. Just upstream from here, past some sheep pens, is an area of flat land known as Rhos-y-Beddau. Here, partly hidden from view by moorland vegetation, is a row of standing stones and a stone circle, one of the few in Wales, and thought to date to the Bronze Age.

From the confluence you now head north up the hillside on the right side of the stream into the attractive and shallow side valley of Cwm Rhiawiau, which cuts into moorland Berwyn. This upper moor consists of thick, deep heather, which makes exploration of the area very difficult. A faint path continues up through the heather to join another path coming up from the right along the broad ridge north of Pistyll Rhaeadr.

The boggy path soon leads to the rounded, unimpressive top of Moel Sych (the dry peak) at 827m/2713 feet, marked by a small cairn at a junction of fences situated on the border of Powys and Clwyd; the remaining high peaks of the range all stand in the county of Clwyd. From the summit you get an excellent view north-east across to the craggy and prominent top of Cadair Berwyn, which gives its name to the whole range.

On a clear day from here you can look to the western skyline with its great arc of hills stretching from Cadair Idris to the Snowdon massif. To the north are the Clywdian hills, and east lie the diminishing ridges of the border hills, the Shropshire plain, the Long Mynd and the Stiperstones, which act as a distant hazy background to a series of beautiful lush, green valleys sweeping down from the Berwyn.

Moel Sych to Pistyll Rhaeadr

The main ridge is easily followed from Moel Sych to Cadair Berwyn (Berwyn's seat), its summit at 827m/2713 feet crowned by a trig point and a refuge circle of stones, which provide a great place for lunch. Although the vegetated and peat-hagged western slopes of these two hills are smooth and gentle, their eastern flanks consist of steep, broken cliffs. A path clings along the edge of these, from where you get exhilarating views down to the dark waters of Llyn Lluncaws, cradled in a hollow below the north-eastern spur of Moel Sych.

If time permits, it's worth an out-and-back trip along to Cadair Bronwen (Bronwen's seat), adding about 5km/3 miles to the outing. The broad ridge continues north over gentle rises and dips with an ever-present fence clinging to its crest, and a line of broken cliffs and scree to the east overlooking a small forest plantation at the head of Cwm Maen Gwynedd. The ridge eventually descends to Bwlch Maen Gwynedd, crossed by an ancient trackway, before climbing to Cadair Bronwen, on whose top at 784m/2572 feet, sits a huge cairn of stones, which are supposed to mark one of the many legendary sites of King Arthur's Table. Beyond Cadair Bronwen, the ridge becomes more open as it sweeps north-west down to Llandrillo and the Dee Valley.

Retracing the ridge back to Moel Sych you now follow its steep though easy eastern spur, down to the southern end of Llyn Luncaws. From the lake, a path crosses the Nant y Llyn stream, and then continues down a narrow valley, its slopes covered in bracken. Eventually the path turns sharp right at a junction of paths to re-cross the stream. As you approach the end of the walk, the air is once again filled with the roar of Pistyll Rhaeadr.

INFORMATION
Start/Finish: The car park beside the waterfall, GR:073295.
Distance: 12km/7½ miles
Walking Time/total climb: 5 hours/650m (2100 feet).
Grading: Moderate; reasonable footpaths over moorland terrain; difficult route finding in bad weather.
Maps: OS Explorer 239, Lake Vyrnwy & Llanfyllin and 255, Llangollen and Berwyn.
Refreshments: Café beside the car park.
Transport: There is no public transport.

Approaching Cadair Berwyn from the south.

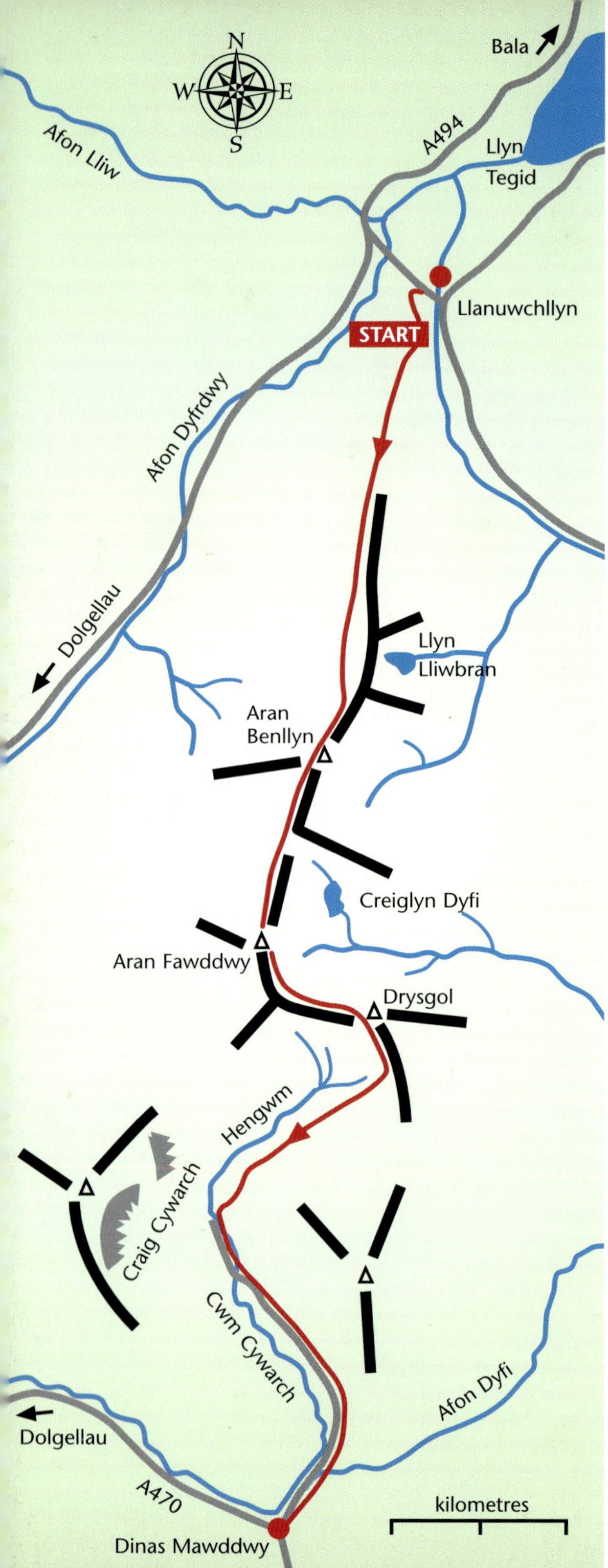

Aran Fawddwy and Aran Benllyn are the two main summits on the rugged Aran ridge and can be approached from either Cwm Cywarch to the south, or from the north starting at the village of Llanuwchllyn at the southern end of Llyn Tegid (Bala Lake). Both walks, though equally rewarding, involve reversing the approach route. However, if transport difficulties can be overcome, then the finest way of tackling the Aran range is to traverse it from end to end. This high-level outing provides one of the finest ridge walks south of the Snowdon massif.

By starting the traverse from Llanuwchllyn, you have a more gradual ascent, with ever-expanding views opening up with every step. This walk also provides a secluded escape for hillgoers wanting to escape from the crowds on the more popular hills around Snowdon.

Llanuwchllyn to Aran Fawddwy

Just south of the village of Llanuwchllyn there is a small car parking area and picnic site near the bridge at Pont y Pandy. A footpath sign points the way down a farm lane running parallel with the Afon Twrch for about 800m/875 yards where a bridleway sign at a stile – the first of many – directs you right, up through grassy fields towards the long, easy-angled spur rising ahead to the south.

Height is steadily gained up the concessionary path by a fence. The path weaves a torturous line along the broad undulating ridge, made up of a series of individual subsidiary tops, each one deceiving you into thinking you've actually reached the summit of Aran Benllyn. Views gradually open up to the west across the Bala Trench to the rugged, twin-tops of Rhobell Fawr and Dduallt rising above the remote, tree-cloaked slopes, with the tops of the Rhinogau just peeping over the col between them. Further right stands the conspicuous dome of Arenig Fawr, which leads the eye down the full length of Bala Lake.

The impressive cliffs of Craig Cywarch.

Crossing Aran Benllyn.

Looking north from the summit of Aran Fawddwy.

*The view from Aran Fawddwy
down to Creiglyn Dyfi.*

At the minor top of Moel Ffenigl you get your first real view of the dramatic eastern slopes stretching from Aran Benllyn to Aran Fawddwy about 3km/2 miles to the south. Just beyond this minor top, the eastern side of the ridge drops sheer down the impressive grey cliffs of Gist Ddu to Llyn Lliwbran, the headwaters of the Afon Twrch, which flows through the meadows of Cwm Cynllwyd.

Ahead, a well-defined footpath now twists its way through grassy hollows dotted with small pools, and over or round a scattering of quartz-streaked crags and boulders to a plateau sheltering a small lake, Llyn Pen Aran. The summit of Aran Benllyn (high ridge above the head of the lakes), marked by a small cairn at 885m/2904 feet, lies a short distance further south.

As you continue south along the broad, rocky ridge you get an excellent birds-eye-view, especially from the minor rise of Erw y Ddafad-ddu, down the grey, quartz-flecked broken cliffs to dark waters of Creiglyn Dyfi, birthplace of the famous Afon Dyfi (or River Dovey). The trig point at the summit of Aran Fawddwy (the high ridge of Mawddwy) is soon reached, which, at 905m/2969 feet is the highest mountain south of the Snowdon range.

On a clear day from beside the trig point, which is set in a plinth of boulders, there is a panoramic feast of distant hills on which to gorge yourself, with the Arenig and Cadair Idris to the west, the Snowdonia range to the north and the blue-grey outline of the Black Mountains and Brecon Beacons often visible 112km/70 miles away to the south. The near range of grassy hills to the east are crossed by the narrow hill road rising to Bwlch y Groes (the pass of the cross), Wales's highest road pass connecting Llanuwchllyn with Dinas Mawddwy. From this high pass, the dark cliffs and cwms below the twin tops of the Aran ridge are seen at their best.

Aran Fawddwy to Dinas Mawddwy

South of Aran Fawddwy, an obvious cairned path drops across bouldery slopes, which soon change abruptly to grassy ones, sweeping down to the slender neck and little top of Drws Bach (little door). Here a cairn commemorates a member of the RAF St

Athan Mountain Rescue Team killed by lightning here in 1960. You have stunning views from here into Cwm Hengwm on the south side, and the rugged east faces of the two main Aran summits to the north.

The path continues east over the smooth spur to the minor top of Drysgol, at the head of Cwm Hengwm, then swings south down boggy ground towards Waun Goch, before slanting across the steep grassy north flanks of Pen yr Allt Uchaf into the classic, ice-carved valley of Cwm Cywarch. This is a lovely place overlooked by the humpy mass of Craig Cywarch with its numerous vegetated crags.

A road in the valley bottom is eventually reached and the walk ends as it started along narrow lanes surrounded by hedgerows, pastureland and wooded slopes leading pleasantly in a about 4km/2½ miles, into the village of Dinas Mawddwy. You will certainly be left with lasting memories of this wild and beautiful corner of Wales.

Looking west from the slopes of Aran Benllyn to Rhobell Fawr and Dduallt.

Gentle hills sweep east from the Aran ridge.

Arenig Fawr reflected in Llyn Celyn.

This outing takes in Arenig Fawr (greater upland), considered by many walkers to be one of the hidden gems of Snowdonia. Mainly due to its solitary position and the way it dominates the surrounding wild and wet moorland, it is a mountain you cannot ignore. Also because of this isolation you get incredible views from its summit. Its craggy profile also makes it a familiar sight for miles around and is perhaps seen at its best from beside the A4212 Bala-Ffestiniog road on a calm, sunny morning reflected in the waters of Llyn Celyn. During the walk you have the option of climbing Moel Llyfnant, Arenig Fawr's near neighbour.

In 1854 when George Borrow first saw Arenig Fawr, he wrote in his *Wild Wales* that he found 'something majestic in its bulk' and 'of all the hills which I saw in Wales, none made a greater impression on me.' Many walkers who ascend Arenig Fawr will agree with Borrow.

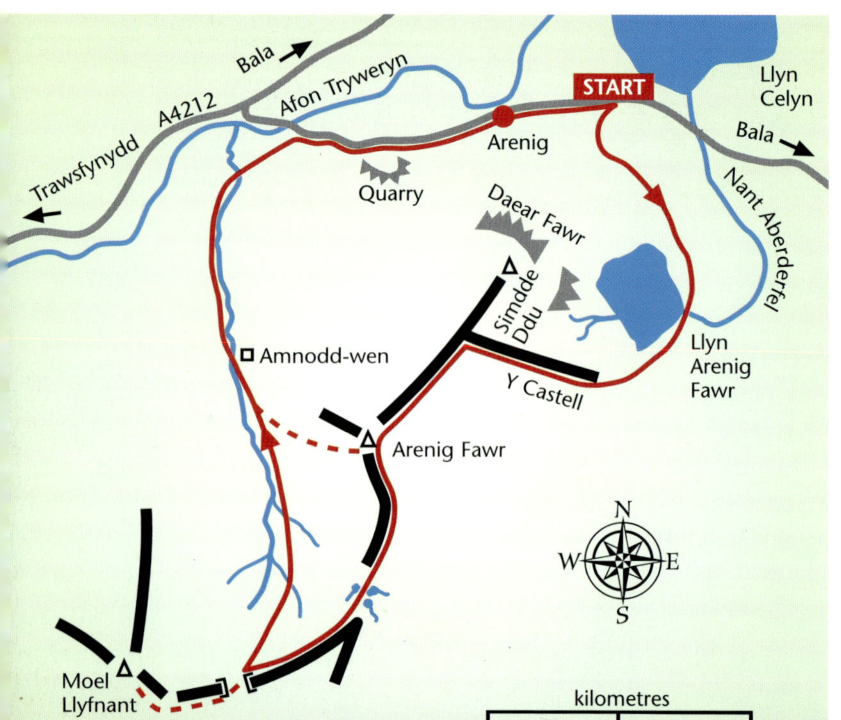

The old Bala road to Arenig Fawr

A convenient starting point is a small roadside parking area opposite a gate on the south side of the minor Trawsfynydd to Bala road, a short distance east of Arenig hamlet and south of Llyn Celyn. Alternatively you can park about 1.5km/1 mile further west at the old quarry below the impressive buttresses of Daear Fawr. Once over a stile beside the gate, a stony track climbs up to Llyn Arenig Fawr arriving at an old dam wall, sluice house and small hut on its eastern edge. The lake is overlooked by a dramatic backcloth of frowning ridges and terraced crags.

After crossing the outflow stream, a faint path climbs the steep grass and heather-cloaked flank of Arenig Fawr passing close to the edge of the rocky outcrop of Carreg Lefain with lovely views down to

98

the reservoir on your right. The path continues up the ridge which rises enticingly alongside the edge of Y Castell with a few deviations right to scramble up some rocky ribs and slabs if the mood takes you.

At the top of the grassy ridge, beyond the subsidiary top of Y Castell, the path continues, crossing two wire fences, to eventually swing right up to more level terrain near Bwlch Blaen-y-nant. The summit is now in view some distance up to the left. A faint path curls left across the south-east face of the mountain gradually climbing and running parallel but below the main ridge. This path is eventually left for a very steep ascent up grassy slopes onto the ridge, where a path, alongside a fence, can be followed to the summit. A less strenuous way though, is to aim directly for the ridge immediately above the second fence then turn left for the summit cone, its high point at 854m/2802 feet. In misty weather the fence, and later a line of posts, provide a useful navigation aid.

Just beside the summit trig point and wind shelter is a memorial to an American crew of a B-29 Flying Fortress bomber, which crashed into the cloud-covered mountain just below the summit on August 4, 1943 with the loss of all the crew. The hollow below the memorial contains remnants of the wreckage.

Arenig Fawr's lofty summit position overlooking the surrounding countryside certainly ensures that on a clear day you are going to be rewarded by stunning views. You can let your eyes roam over most of the hills of North and Central Wales and maybe even glimpse the sea off Colwyn Bay to the north. You will certainly pick out the popular peaks of Snowdon and the Glyderau, while nearer at hand to the north, across the main Bala road, lies Arenig Fach and the Migneint. To the south-east is Llyn Tegid backed by the Hirnant hills and the distant Berwyn range. To the west is the shapely profile of Moel Llyfnant, the near neighbour of Arenig Fawr.

Arenig Fawr to the old Bala road

The easiest descent from the summit is to return by the route you came. Alternatively, a short walk south leads down to a col from where you can head north-north-west down into the valley to the west of Arenig Fawr and then follow a track back to the

Arenig Fawr rises above Llyn Arenig Fawr.

Steep slopes sweep up Y Castell above Llyn Arenig Fawr.

Approaching the summit of Arenig Fawr.

road. However, a more interesting and challenging descent, albeit a longer one, is to follow Arenig Fawr's south ridge and then eventually descend the same valley as above. This allows you the option of ascending the neighbouring hill of Moel Llyfnant.

Once across the col, just below the main summit of Arenig Fawr, its subsidiary top is soon reached from where you can look down the long knobbly southern ridge to a collection of small lakes. Continuing south down the broad ridge, scree gives way to grass. Eventually you arrive at a secluded area of crags, knolls and a scattering of small lakes sheltering beneath the bulky flanks of Arenig Fawr. A steep descent south-west alongside a wall takes you down to the exposed and marshy col between Arenig Fawr and Moel Llyfnant.

If you want to ascend Moel Llyfnant then a steep trudge up and back down its east face, mainly over rough, trackless terrain beyond the broad col, is the obvious way. Alternatively, you can miss out Moel Llyfnant and opt for the easier option which follows a good track heading north. This leads down the valley past a forestry plantation, from where a waymarked path passes through the ruins of Amnodd-wen farm. Beyond here the path becomes boggy until you reach a track, which soon veers north-east to give pleasant walking alongside the track bed of the old GWR railway. On reaching the road you simply follow it right, back to the starting point.

The steep cliffs of Daear Fawr on the eastern flanks of Arenig Fawr.

INFORMATION
Start/Finish: Small lay-by opposite a gate situated just east of Arenig village, alongside the minor Bala to Trawsfynydd road; GR: 846396. Alternative start is a car park about 1.5km/1 mile further west by a disused quarry; GR: 831393.
Distance: 17.5km/11 miles.
Walking Time/total climb: 6 hours/525m (1722 feet); slightly longer if Moel Llyfnant is included.
Grading: Difficult; some good footpaths but with trackless sections through a rugged and remote mountain area.
Maps: OS Explorer OL18.
Refreshments: Nearest cafes and pubs in Bala.
Transport: No public transport to the starting point.

Arenig Fawr and Moel Llyfnant on the skyline across the Migneint.

WALK 17   THE MIGNEINT AND ARENIG FACH

This walk explores the vast area of windswept moorland known as the Migneint, which stretches north-east from Ffestiniog to Ysbyty Ifan and south to Llyn Celyn. It is a remote and wild landscape of heather, peat hags and bogs, set in a shallow depression with gentle, higher ground almost encircling it.

The source of the name Migneint is 'mignen', which means a morass, and on Migneint you find the largest expanse of blanket bog in Wales; it is also some of the finest in Europe. While on the drier areas are to be found heather, wispy cotton-grass, bilberry and grasses. Overlooking the moor from the east is the dominant peak of Arenig Fach, which, in certain lighting conditions, takes on the appearance of a hill of much greater stature and seems much further away.

Due to its lack of obvious landmark features, strength-sapping bogs, and few footpaths venturing through its knobbly tussocks and deep heather, the Migneint has acquired a harsh reputation among walkers. This is particularly true in wet and misty weather, or in deep snow, when good navigation skills are a prerequisite for a crossing.

However, this reputation is really unfounded and if you pick a dry, clear day for the crossing, you can stride out below broad skies. Then you will experience a unique circuit through some of the most evocative scenery in this part of Wales. You are still likely to get wet feet, but it's nowhere near as difficult as a crossing of say Kinder Scout or Bleaklow in the Peak District. Once experienced, the crossing of the Migneint lasts long in the memory.

The highlight of the walk is the wonderful view from the summit of Arenig Fach back across the patchy, boggy moorland of the Migneint. On the walk you will see a wide range of bog plants and moorland birds, particularly red grouse, wheatear and skylark.

Conwy Road to Arenig Fach

The walk starts from a small car parking spot beside a bridge at GR 774440, beside the unfenced Ffestiniog to Pentrefoelas road. From here a faint path leads south-east up the north bank of a small stream onto the heather moor. After about 600m/655 yards you need to swing right (south) across some peat hags and black, slimy groughs full of bogs. Watch out for the patches of bright green sphagnum moss – you could sink up to your waist in these. Ahead is the rocky mound of Cerrig Llwynogod crowned by an obvious slate obelisk silhouetted against the skyline.

From beside the slate tablet, with a letter 'E' carved on it and set among quartz-dappled rocks, you get your first real view across the vast morass of the Migneint. Down to the right is Llyn Serw, one of only two lakes on the Migneint. Beyond Llyn Serw is the shapely peak of Moel Llyfnant, joined by a low pass to Arenig Fawr, and further left is the aloof Arenig Fach, the main physical feature on this vast area of moorland. Just peeping over the left shoulder of Arenig Fach is the distant Carnedd y Filiast (cairn of the greyhound bitch). Back to the west the craggy Moelwyn hills look superb while to the north is Llyn Conwy whose waters feed the infant Afon Conwy.

Our way now lies south-west along a broad moorland ridge. Leaving behind the rocky mound, a small cairn is passed before dropping down to a boggy col, beyond which a faint path heads along the ridge, with heather slopes down to the left and grassy slopes leading gently down to Llyn Serw. The ridge gives pleasant walking with Arenig Fach dominating the view ahead. Another cairn is passed at spot height 479m (1572ft), just before reaching a ladder stile and gate at a wire fence.

Approaching Cerrig Llwynogod.

The view west from Cerrig Llwynogod to the Moelwyn hills.

Looking south across the boggy hollow of the Migneint to Llyn Serw.

Approaching the Afon Serw with Arenig Fach on the skyline ahead.

Just beyond the stile a path, really a sheep trod, contours south down a marshy, depression to Cefngarw, its chimney pots visible above the grassy rise ahead.

As you cross a grassy knoll the isolated farmstead of Cefngarw, surely one of the loneliest dwellings in Wales, suddenly comes into view. The buildings are used during sheep gatherings and are usually approached along a 5km/3 mile track climbing up from the north-east above the Afon Serw. Beyond the dwelling sits Arenig Fach towering over the marshy hollow of the Migneint through which the Afon Serw winds its sinewy way north-east. A crossing of the river is the next obstacle.

Descending east from Cefngarw, a wall and some ancient sheep pens are passed on their left, beyond which grassy slopes lead down to gate in a wire fence. You soon arrive at a sharp bend in the Afon Serw below a craggy knoll on the opposite side of the river. Unless the river is in spate, when you can expect wet feet, large boulders usually provide a reasonably dry crossing. Ahead now lies a steady climb east across deep heather slopes with the occasional sheep trod for company up to the cairn at Carnedd y Gors-gam (GR: 813417). A steep ascent up the western flanks of Arenig Fach (lesser upland) lands you on the heather-covered summit plateau, with a trig point and stone shelter at 689m/2260 feet.

From the summit of Arenig Fach you look west across the Migneint and south-east to the near-neighbour of Arenig Fawr. However, it is the view obtained a short distance to the east, which comes as a surprise. For here you can peer down the steep cliffs on Arenig Fach's rocky east face to the dark waters of Llyn Arenig Fach, situated in a hollow high above walled sheep pastures and backed by broad moorland slopes sweeping round to Carnedd y Filiast.

Arenig Fach to the Conwy Road

Leaving the lofty summit perch of Arenig Fach, its southern ridge is followed for a short distance before heading west down rough heathery slopes to meet a series of boundary stones leading towards the broad col and pile of stones at Cerrig y Bala. Heading out south-west, the rough slopes of the broad ridge are climbed past more boundary stones at Carnedd y Fran before reaching the summit of Carnedd Iago at 538m/1765 feet, the second highest point of the walk and a great vantage point for admiring the arc of encircling hills.

The going now becomes easier and a faint path leads north-west along the edge of a forest plantation, which has crept up the slopes over recent years. Beyond the woods a procession of boundary stones point the way north-west for about a kilometre/2/3 mile before you head west to Llyn Dywarchen situated in a shallow hollow. By heading north from here across peat hags and rough heather moorland you regain the road near Rhyd Cerig Gwynion and then follow it right to the small bridge and the end of the walk.

INFORMATION
Start/Finish: Roadside car park by a small bridge at GR: 774440, 700m/765 yards south-west of Pont ar Gonwy on the unfenced B4407 Ffestiniog to Pentrefoelas road. No public transport to this point.
Distance: 19km/12 miles.
Walking Time/total climb: 6 hours/254m (835 feet).
Grading: Very Difficult; a demanding walk across mainly rough, trackless heather moorland. Best avoided during periods of wet weather. Good navigation skills are essential in misty conditions.
Maps: OS OL18.
Refreshments: Pubs and cafes in Ffestiniog and Bala.

Above: *Arenig Fach dominates the Migneint landscape.*

Left: *The isolated farmstead of Cefngarw in the heart of the Migneint, with Arenig Fach on the skyline.*

The Dyfi hills overlooking Dinas Mawddwy.

WALK 18   THE DYFI HILLS

This walk crosses the gentle, moorland Dyfi hills, which are linked by narrow cols. These quiet hills, whose tops straddle the long undulating ridge extending east from the rocky slopes of Cadair Idris to Dinas Mawddwy, offer pleasant walking, mainly along faint paths, through a usually deserted landscape.

As they drive west along the A470 over Bwlch Oerddrws on their way to Dolgellau maybe with thoughts focused on an ascent of Cadair Idris, how many walkers give the rolling green hills on the left more than a passing glance? Although the tops are smooth and grassy, their northern flanks are etched deeply by a series of wild, dramatic cwms such as Cwm Cerist, which bites deeply into the range. By contrast, the steep-sided cwms and ridges on the southern slopes are cloaked in dense forest but thankfully the summit ridges – several over 610m/2000 feet in height – have survived afforestation.

Although the ridge can be walked in either direction, on sunny days the preferred choice is east to west when the light captures the best features of these hills. Either way a traverse of the Dyfi Hills will guarantee a memorable day out, with the added advantage of both ends of the walk being linked by a regular bus service.

Dinas Mawddwy to Cribin Fawr

The usual starting point is a lane which leaves the A470 (GR: 848154), about 1km/2/3 mile north-west of Dinas Mawddwy. The lane leads left to Ty'n-y-braich Farm overlooked by the brooding crags along the rim of Craig Maesglase. The shimmering cascades of a fine waterfall tumble down a series of rocky steps on Craig Maesglase on its way to the

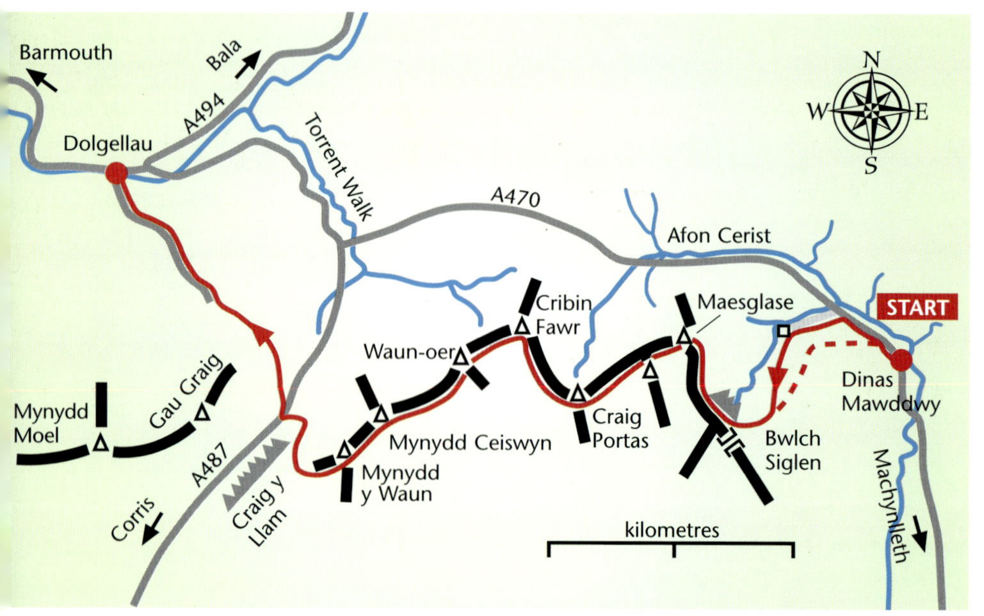

sylvan Gulcwm valley below. The falls are a real spectacle after heavy rain, and in autumn the bracken-covered slopes at the back of the cwm glow a golden brown.

Just before the road starts to descend to the farm, leave it through a gate on the left into a field where a footpath climbs up to Bwlch Siglen. This bwlch (col) can also be reached from a lay-by (GR: 857150) near Dinas Mawddwy. A zigzag footpath leads up through woods, eventually contouring around the grassy slopes of Ffridd Gulcwm from where you get a fine view across to Maesglase Falls.

The paths merge near Bwlch Siglen and continue along the very rim of Craig Maesglase's brooding cliffs, from where you get a close-up view of the waterfall and can gaze over Gulcwm's green, chequered fields. Pleasant walking over the heathery plateau leads up to the summit of Maesglase (blue meadow). At 674m/ 2211feet, this is the high point of the ridge although the highest ground actually lies on Maen Du, a jutting promontory just to the north-east from where you can gaze across the A470 to Cwm Cywarch backed by the Aran hills.

A path, now paralleled by a wire fence – a useful guide in misty conditions – swings gently south-west and descends across a carpet of mossy turf and heather towards a slight dip just before the top of Craig Portas is reached. The shattered north facing slopes of Craig Portas, overlooking the green depths of Cwm Cerist, impart an almost impregnable appearance to the peak. Along this part of the walk you can gaze south across the Dyfi Forest towards Pumlumon (or Plynlimon) and the distant sea, while north lie the Aran hills, Rhobell Fawr and the lovely pyramid-shaped Dduallt, backed by Arenig Fawr and Arenig Fach.

Above left: Approaching Bwlch Siglen, with Maesglase in the background.

Above right: Heading for Craig Maesglase.

The rounded hills at the southern end of the Aran range seen from the approach to Maeslase.

Above left: *The escarpment of Craig Maesglase with its dramatic waterfall.*

Above right: *Crossing the top of Craig Maesglase.*

From Craig Portas the rocky escarpment swings north towards the equally impressive and craggy Cribin Fawr. Ahead now lies an entertaining section of the walk, which involves a steep descent overlooking the shattered rim of Cwm Cerist to a shallow depression where the infant Afon Cerist rises at the start of its short but interesting journey to its confluence with the Afon Dyfi at Dinas Mawddwy. Beyond the hanging valley a faint path leads up easy slopes to the edge of the crags and Cribin Fawr's summit at 659m/2132 feet from where you get a fine vista back across Cwm Cerist to craggy Maesglase.

Cribin Fawr to Dolgellau

The ridge now swings west and the path stays with the fence, descending steeply to the saddle where you can look down into the conifer plantations, which in recent years have spread up the higher slopes of Cwm Ceiswyn almost to the ridge. A steep climb takes you up to the top of Wauen-oer complete with mast and trig point. Like most of the hills on this walk, Wauen-oer at 670m/2197 feet is a rounded lump when viewed from the south, but by contrast, broken cliffs rim its east-facing cwm. On a clear day you can look south-west to Cadair Idris whose dramatic profile dominates the skyline. Wauen-oer gives one of the best viewpoints for the ice-carved Cwm Cau.

A snowstorm sweeps across the Dyfi hills.

Continuing in the same direction, close to the edge of the wood on your left, the minor top of Mynydd Ceiswyn is crossed en-route to the hump of Mynydd y Waun just above the forest boundary. After a steep, grassy descent north-west you meet the metalled lane coming up from Aberllefenni.

Beyond the lane, grassy slopes give access up to the summit of Craig y Llam from where you have superb views across to Cadair Idris and down the valley to Tal-y-llyn lake. A grassy ridge along the top of the broken cliffs of Craig y Llam now descends gently to a wall from where a path drops down left through a small gorge. The path ends near a large lay-by a short distance below the high point on the A487 Dolgellau-Machynlleth road.

If two cars have been used then the outing can end here. Otherwise, you walk up the road for 300m/330 yards and cross a stile on the left, from where a good path traverses round the northern tip of Cadair Idris. The path passes below the rocky nose of Gau Graig to the road head at Bwlch-coch. It is now only a short road walk into the centre of Dolgellau to catch the bus back to Dinas Mawddwy.

INFORMATION

Start/finish: Dinas Mawddwy; GR: 848154

Distance: 21km/12 miles.

Walking Time/total climb: 6 hours/ 1200m (3940 feet).

Grading: Moderate; an easy but exposed walk over mainly grassy and heather-clad hills. Difficult in misty conditions.

Maps: OS Explorer OL 23.

Refreshments: The Red Lion, Dinas Mawddwy and various pubs and cafes in Dolgellau.

Transport: Buses between Dolgellau and Aberangell.

Above: *Cadair Idris dominates the view west from Craig y Llam.*

Left: *Looking north-east from Maesglase across Gulcwm Valley to the Aran hills.*

Typical Rhinog terrain on the approach to Llyn Hywel from Cwm Nantcol.

The Dyffryn burial chamber.

7 THE RUGGED RHINOGAU

The Rhinog range (or Y Rhinogau), rise in an undulating skyline running for 32km/20 miles from the Vale of Ffestiniog in the north to the Mawddach Estuary, in the south. They are seen in all their glory from the Trawsfynydd to Dolgellau road. These are the same hills, which in the twelfth century, Giraldus Camrensis described as the 'roughest and harshest district in all Wales'. Most walkers who have traversed this range will probably agree with these sentiments for their gentle appearance belies the true nature of the Rhinogau. It is an unspoilt and wild landscape loved by walkers who want to escape the hustle and bustle of the over-crowded hills to the north. The twin peaks of Rhinog Fawr and Rhinog Fach name the range – the Rhinogau.

Now protected as the Rhinog National Nature Reserve, this is a land of many contrasts. To the east the land slopes away in grassy moorland, much of it now cloaked in uniform plantations of Sitka spruce. Although there are easy ways into the hills from the east, it is the western flanks which offer the finest approaches. Here you will find natural woodlands, impressive cwms and hidden lakes. Further west is Cardigan Bay, where are found some of the most beautiful dune-scapes in Snowdonia and the northern coastal area ends with Edward I's spectacular Harlech Castle.

The Rhinog geology is unlike that of the volcanic mountains to the north. Here are to be found the bare bones of an ancient and weather-beaten landscape consisting of the thickest (2000m/6560 feet) layer of Cambrian sediments in Britain, formed more than 500 million years ago. The rocks were folded to produce a giant dome known as the Harlech Dome. Here are to be found grits, shales and slates, with the texture of some of the sandstone outcrops resembling the much younger millstone grit of the Peak District and Yorkshire.

What has been left behind is a wild, rugged place for lovers of solitude. Never rising above 756m/2480 feet, the Rhinog mountain range is like a big-dipper whose slopes

110

Rhinog Fawr and Rhinog Fach at the head of Cwm Nantcol.

Llyn Hywel backed by Rhinog Fach.

Approaching the summit of Y Llethr.

are covered in terraces and boulder fields cloaked in a carpet of bilberry and heather. This makes the terrain, especially in the northern section, difficult, unrelenting and unforgiving for the careless walker.

Nowhere in Wales are rocks so contorted and roughly strewn. This mixture of rocky ridges, low passes and ever-changing views of mountain, moor, sea and coastline, provides magnificent but challenging walking country. To traverse the complete Rhinogau ridge in a single day is one of Britain's finest walks, and one which demands fitness and good navigation skills. For most walkers though the shorter routes up Rhinog Fawr and Rhinog Fach are sufficient attractions. By contrast the hills at the southern end of the range are smooth and grassy, where you can stride out easily.

Rhinog Fach and Rhinog Fawr are separated by the prominent gap of Bwlch Drws Ardudwy, the high point of a narrow, crag-lined defile, which has a fascinating history and is part of the 400ha/990 acres of the National Nature Reserve. The Rhinogau cut off the strip of land along the coast, known as Ardudwy, from the rest of Wales. The men of Ardudwy, a group of treacherous brigands, would travel through the pass to raid the land beyond the Rhinog peaks of Fawr and Fach (the big and small gateposts), then returning with stolen cattle and other goods to their coastal hideaway. The pass of Drws Ardudwy has probably changed little since those prehistoric days, and the steep slopes either side are just as daunting now as they must have been to those early travellers.

In fact this whole coastal area, especially Ardudwy, is rich in historical associations. The northern part of the Rhinogau was highly populated throughout the Iron and Bronze Ages and scattered across the area are various hut circles, ancient cairns, stone circles, burial chambers and old hill forts. Examples include the stone circle at Bryn Cader Farer to the north-west of Foel Penolau, the Dyffryn burial chamber, a Neolithic site dating back to 3-4000 BC, in the village of Dyffryn Ardudwy, and the hill-top Iron Age fort at Craig y Dinas.

Although walkers are attracted to Rhinog Fawr and Rhinog Fach, neither of these two peaks, which are among the roughest in the Rhynogau, is the highest point; this honour goes to Y Llethr just to the south, and even the rounded dome of Diffwys whose long, gentle grassy ridge reaches down to Barmouth, is higher. By contrast, the lower hills at the northern end of the range are much more rugged, with the little-visited section between Clip and Foel Penolau being particularly wild and attractive. Here you can pioneer pathless ways to rocky summits and scramble up unnamed rocky outcrops in a landscape very reminiscent of the Rough Bounds of Knoydart in Scotland.

Many walkers approach the Rhinogau from the west, usually from the road head at either Cwm Nantcol or Cwm Bychan. Both these exquisite places are reached along narrow, twisting roads that rise up from the coast road at Llanbedr, passing through a landscape thickly cloaked in oak and birch which soon gives way to pastureland patterned by walled fields.

The popular centres for exploring this area are Barmouth and Harlech, where there are numerous B&Bs, hotels and campsites. Both towns are served by the Cambrian Coastal Railway, which runs between Porthmadog and Machynlleth. There are also useful campsites at Tal-y-bont and just off the Cwm Bychan road.

Rugged terrain on the slopes of Rhinog Fach.

The sand dunes at Harlech.

The small bridge below the Roman steps.

This demanding and exciting circular walk starts at Cwm Bychan and explores part of the wild northern region of the Rhinog range. The walk then continues south across the complex and hostile terrain of Craig Wion to Rhinog Fawr, finally returning to Cwm Bychan via the Roman Steps. Although a relatively short walk, it is difficult in places, with faint paths winding around unnamed rocky bluffs, dipping in and out of rocky canyons and crossing boulder fields cloaked in dense heather. This unique rocky landscape with its hidden lakes and boulder-strewn slopes offers an adventurous trip through some of the wildest scenery in North Wales.

The walk starts from the road head at beautiful Cwm Bychan. Here, set in hollow lies Llyn Cwm Bychan overlooked by rough, tumbling crags, on the impressive Careg-y-Saeth (rock of the arrows) which act as a fine foreground for a view of Rhinog Fawr.

Cwm Bychan to Rhinog Fawr

From the farm buildings at the end of the road, a path climbs steeply north to join another path coming up from the left, which then continues diagonally upwards as it crosses the hillside towards Clip and the obvious col on the skyline ahead. Along this section you have splendid views south to Rhinog Fawr and the nearer flat-topped Craig Wion, with its terraced cliffs and rocky outcrops cut by deep trenches. The area around Clip is a wilderness of rock and heather. To the north, Clip's rocky summit ridge linking Moel Ysgyfarnogod, is really a jumble of slabby sheets of grey rock littered with heather-covered boulders, rocky steps and numerous summits. It is a confusing and complex terrain which in poor visibility becomes a trap for the unwary.

114

The path continues around Clip towards Bwlch Gwylim and the crags of Craig Ddrwg. Just before reaching the top of the pass a transverse wall is reached. Here the main path continues on to Llyn Trawsfynydd, but our way is now south-east towards the rocky tops of Craig Wion and the main spine of the Rhinogau.

The easy part is now over and the challenging part of the walk begins. A faint path weaves its way through heather and boulders and involves some scrambling over several rocky outcrops before the cairned summit of Craig Wion is finally reached.

Here you can see the shimmering waters of Llyn Pryfed and Llyn Twr-glas set amid huge horizontal slabs of rock and heather down to your left. To the south the undulating rocky ridge of Craig Wion leads towards Rhinog Fawr, while to the north-east you can pick out Llyn Trawsfynydd with its infamous Magnox power station, now closed and awaiting decommissioning.

Ahead now lies the most complex part of the ridge through a twisted rocky landscape of boulders, heather-cloaked crags and numerous gorges. This area was memorably-described by Harold Drasdo in *Big Walks* as 'a mile of Celtic badlands'. The contours shown on the OS 1:25000 scale map don't really prepare you for the up-and-down terrain which lies ahead. You scramble in and out of numerous ravines which cross the ridge and pass beneath some impressive crags. In misty weather this section is a navigator's nightmare. Any paths you do find are followed in the general direction of Rhinog Fawr. Soon after catching a view of Llyn Morwynion down to your right, you pass below a huge crag and descend to Bwlch Tyddiad where you meet a good path rising up via the Roman Steps from Cwm Bychan, the only easy approach into this area.

After crossing over the pass and descending to the east, a narrower path leads right, weaving its way through boulders and sinewy heather up to Llyn Du (the black lake), a small and isolated lake in the shadow of the terraced buttresses of Rhinog Fawr's north face. Veer from the path and the going becomes very difficult.

The lakeside is an idyllic spot for a refreshment break and to try and work out how to get up the steep face. The most direct route is from the far shore of the lake where

Llyn Cwm Bychan overlooked by Castell Careg-y-saeth.

Looking down on Gloyw Llyn from the slopes of Rhinog Fawr.

The rocky shoreline of Llyn Du.

a scree gully slants up right, eventually joining steep, scree-covered paths climbing left up the north-western flanks of Rhinog Fawr to its summit trig point and cairn at 720m/2362 feet. Alternatively you can stay on the boulder-strewn north shore of the lake and continue ahead up an easier path which climbs west to a wall. Continuing alongside the wall a cairned path soon weaves a way left up the slopes to where a short section of scree lands you at the rocky summit.

Whichever route is taken the views from the small rounded rocky summit cloaked in heather and bilberry are excellent, especially south across Bwlch Drws Ardudwy to Rhinog Fach and Y Llethr beyond, with Llyn Hywel, one of the Rhinog gems, just visible in the dip between them.

Above: *The 'badlands' of Craig Wion across Cwm Bychan.*

Right: *Pleasant walking towards Clip.*

Rhinog Fawr to Cwm Bychan

Retracing your steps down the easier approach route for Rhinog Fawr you eventually arrive at a stile crossing a wall level with Llyn Du. The path continues alongside the wall overlooking the lake and crosses rocky terrain before descending steeply to meet the main path below Bwlch Tyddiad. Turning left here the path drops down to the Roman Steps.

The age of these worn and polished flagstones has been debated for years but it is generally thought – mainly due to the spacing of the slabs – that despite their name, they were part of a medieval packhorse route. Occasionally the steps disappear but the route is always obvious as you descend through heather, eventually crossing a small hump-backed bridge. Beyond here the path passes through rowan trees and a belt of ancient oak woodland before descending to the car park in Cwm Bychan.

Descending the Roman steps.

Looking across Cwm Bychan to Rhinog Fawr.

Clip dominates the view at the head of Cwm Bychan.

INFORMATION
Start/Finish: The car park at the eastern end of Llyn Cwm Bychan; GR: 647314. (small fee).
Distance: 11km/6 ¾ miles.
Walking Time/total climb: 6 – 8 hours/ 1020m (3345eet).
Grading: Very Difficult; a walk with mainly good paths but with some pathless sections across heather-covered boulder-fields and with numerous rocky outcrops to be passed. Good navigation skills needed in poor visibility.
Maps: OS Explorer OL 18.
Refreshments: Cafes and pubs in Llanbedr and Tal-y-bont.
Transport: No public transport to Cwm Bychan.

The head of Cwm Nantcol.

WALK 20 RHINOG FACH AND Y LLETHR FROM CWM NANTCOL

This excellent skyline circular walk starts at the remote Cwm Nantcol, ascends Rhinog Fach from the narrow, craggy defile of Bwlch Drws Ardudwy (the pass of the door of Ardudwy), then continues south along a magnificent ridge to Y Llethr overlooking the remote waters of Llyn Hywel. From Y Llethr, the highest peak in the Rhinogau, the terrain suddenly changes and gentle grassy slopes are descended back into Cwm Nantcol. The circuit passes through some rugged terrain, there are superb views throughout and fascinating historical associations.

Cwm Nantcol is much wilder and more open that its neighbour Cwm Bychan to the north, and is also approached by a narrow hill road from the coastal village of Llanbedr. The road weaves its way up through ancient woodlands alongside the lively Afon Cwmnantcol and once the woods are left behind, you have an excellent view across upper Cwm Nantcol, whose headwall is dominated by Rhinog Fach and Rhinog Fawr, the two craggy sentinels separated by the V-shaped trench of the Pass of Ardudwy. The road eventually ends at a farm at Maes-y-garnedd.

Maes-y-garnedd was the birthplace of John Jones, an ardent Parliamentarian during the Civil War and husband to Oliver Cromwell's sister Catherine, eventually becoming Commissioner of Parliament for the Government of Ireland. He was also one of the signatories of the death warrant of Charles I at the end of the Civil War. After the Restoration, he was executed for treason along with regicide.

Cwm Nantcol to Rhinog Fach

From Maes-y-garnedd, an obvious signed footpath heads north-east, following the left side of a stone wall through a number of gates, and climbs steadily towards the deep pass of Bwlch Drws Ardudwy. From the path you have an excellent view of the ribbed west face of Rhinog Fach and its conspicuous diagonal bands of rock. This is a wild and isolated area, with Rhinog Fawr closing in behind you on the left and Rhinog Fach to the right.

Eventually you pass the start of a path heading off right up heather-covered slopes to Llyn Hywel and offering an alternative approach to Rhinog Fach. Our way though continues ahead up through a marshy hollow and rocky gorge to reach a prominent cairn at the top of the pass. Bwlch Drws Ardudwy linked the fertile land to the east of the Rhinogau with the coastal plain of Ardudwy, once home to the men of Ardudwy, an infamous group of outlaws and brigands. I wonder if they also appreciated the fine view from here of the eastern skyline filled by the quartet of Arenig Fawr, Moel Lyfnant, Dduallt and Rhobell Fawr?

From the pass a very steep path climbs the rugged, heather-clad slopes directly up Rhinog Fach. The angle eases above the initial pull, and the path then winds its way through numerous rock bands before eventually steepening again to gain a ridge leading to a cairn at the summit of Rhinog Fach at 712m/2333 feet, situated at the end of a wall coming in from the west. From the nearly flat, twin-topped summit, cloaked in heather and bilberries you can look south across the ice-carved, lonely hanging valley cradling Llyn Hywel, to the steep grass slopes and ribbed rock strata of Y Llethr, the highest point on the Rhinogau.

Right: *A magnificent wall clings
to the southern crest of Rhinog Fach.*

Heading towards the Bwlch Drws Ardudwy.

Descending Y Llethr towards Diffwys.

*The craggy Rhinog Fach seen from
the shore of Llyn Hywel.*

INFORMATION
Start/Finish: Car park (small fee) at the end of the road in Cwm Nantcol near Maes-y-garnedd, GR: 642270.
Distance: 15km/9½ miles
Walking Time/total climb: About 6 hours/800m (2600 feet).
Grading: Difficult; mainly on good paths but with some steep scree and heather-covered slopes on Rhinog Fach; it can be very boggy in places.
Maps: OS Explorer OL18.
Refreshments: Cafes and pubs in Llanbeder and Tal-y-bont.
Transport: No public transport.

Rhinog Fach to Cwm Nantcol

To reach the col separating Rhinog Fach and Y Llethr involves a very steep descent down craggy slopes. From the summit cairn you follow the impressive wall as it swings south and plunges down rocky slopes and scree to arrive at a narrow ridge crossing the col. Down to your right is Llyn Hywel where huge tilted slabs plunge into its dark waters.

Continuing alongside the wall, which clings to the rocky crest of the col, an obvious path soon veers away to the right and weaves its way steadily up the steep rock-strewn slopes. Higher up the path rejoins the wall before a grassy area is reached and the nearby modest cairn at the summit of Y Llethr (the steep slope) at 756m/2480 feet. During the final stages of the ascent you have excellent views back across the Y Llethr slabs and Llyn Hywel to the soaring shattered face of Rhinog Fach sweeping up above crags and scree slopes, with Rhinog Fawr peeping over its shoulder.

Typical Rhinog terrain of heather, rocky terraces and boulder fields is now replaced by gentle grassy slopes, although the conspicuous drystone wall – a navigator's friend – which starts on Rhinog Fach, still continues south, virtually unbroken, over Diffwys to within sight of Barmouth and the Mawddach Estuary.

Following the wall downhill to a couple of ladder stiles, the right hand one is crossed, and a sturdy straight wall followed right, down the broad grassy ridge of Moelyblithcwm at the head of Cwm Ysgethin. Llyn Bodlyn is visible down to the left at the foot of the craggy north-west face of Diffwys. Straight ahead is the isolated hill of Moelfre, one of the best vantage points in the area for views across Cwm Nantcol to Rhinog Fach and Rhinog Fawr.

After about 2km/1¼ miles of steady walking – which can be very boggy in places – the wall swings sharp right while the path continues south-west for another 1.2km/¾ mile crossing a col towards the corner of another wall beneath the eastern spur of Moelfre. Continuing along the left side of the wall towards Moelfre you soon reach a stile by a gate.

Once over the wall stile a faint bridleway leads north down towards Cwm Nantcol, passing through several walled pastures until the unfenced road is reached. Turning right here you are accompanied by fine views ahead as the road is followed gently back towards Maes-y-garnedd and the end of the walk.

Right: *Looking up the south ridge of Rhinog Fach.*

Below: *The two Rhinog hills beyond Llyn Hywel from Y Llethr.*

The spectacular Cwm Cau.

*Penygadair, the high point of
the range, seen from Cyfrwy.*

8 CADAIR IDRIS

The small town of Dolgellau, at the head of the narrow straits of the Mawddach Estuary is famous for two things – gold, and the craggy Cadair Idris (or Cader Idris) range. A minor gold rush took place hereabouts in the mid–1800's. For walkers though, Cadair Idris is the real treasure of the area. It is the most southerly mountain group of the Snowdonia National Park and certainly one of its finest and most popular, rivalled only by Snowdon itself. As with Snowdon, it is also exposed to bad weather blowing in from the sea.

Cadair Idris means 'the Chair of Idris' and certainly the scooped Cwm y Gadair looks like a large chair with a back and ridges for arms. It is uncertain where the name came from. Many writers have said that Idris was a legendary giant, while other stories link the name with Idris ap Gwyddno, a Celtic prince who was killed in battle against encroaching Saxons around 630 A.D. The name has even been linked with the legend of Arthur. However, the origin of the name is not really important, what matters to us is that Cadair Idris is a magnificent mountain range.

Cadair Idris is defined to the south-east by the long wooded valley containing Tal-y-llyn Lake (or Llyn Mwyngil) and the Dysynni Valley along which the road leads to the coastal resort of Tywyn. To the north-west, wooded foothills run from the ancient town of Dolgellau along the Mawddach Estuary to the resort of Barmouth. In fact the tremendous north-facing escarpment dominates the view from the estuary and gave rise to the saying that the walls of Dolgellau are a mile high. In reality, with its soaring ridges and ice-carved cwms, Cadair Idris is more of a range than a single peak with the 20km/12 miles ridge containing nine tops over 610m/2000 feet, the highest point being 893m/2930 feet at Penygadair (or Pen y Gadair).

For walkers there are three established approaches to Cadair's summit: from the north by the Pony Path, which starts at the National Park car park at Ty Nant, about 4km/2½ miles west of Dolgellau; from the south by the very steep ascent from

Minffordd via the magnificent Cwm Cau; while for those wanting a quiet and gentler route, then the Dysynni Valley approach from the south-west is very attractive.

Lying 1.5km/1 mile to the south-west of Minffordd is Tal-y-llyn Lake (Llyn Mwyngil) backed by the Tarren hills and set in the deep trench of the 48km/30 miles Bala fault. The lake, formed when a landslide into the valley created a natural dam, has given its name to the railway linking Abergynolwyn, just south-west of the lake, through the delightful wooded Talyllyn Valley to Tywyn at the coast. The famous 2ft-gauge railway, originally used to transport slate to the main railway line at the coast, is thought to be the oldest of its kind in the world, and has been in continuous service since 1867.

There are various centres to explore Cadair Idris from, including Dolgellau, Barmouth and Tywyn, where you will find numerous hotels, B&Bs, campsites and several youth hostels. The area is also reasonably well served by buses.

Cwm Amarch sweeps up above Tal-y-llyn Lake.

Above: *Sunset across the Mawddach Estuary.*

Left: *The lakes of Llynnau Creggenen and Cadair Idris from the west.*

The wooded slopes above Minffordd.

WALK 21 CADAIR IDRIS FROM MINFFORDD

This walk from Minffordd via Cwm Cau is the most spectacular and rewarding way to climb Cadair Idris. Cadair's long main ridge contains a series of craggy, ice-sculptured cwms, some holding exquisite lakes. The most impressive of these is Cwm Cau (the hollow cwm), and is the highlight of this circular walk, which follows well-maintained paths for much of the ascent up to Penygadair, the high point of Cadair Idris.

Minffordd to Penygadair

From the far end of the car park a raised causeway leads through an avenue of chestnut trees then swings left past the Visitor Centre. Just beyond here, a gate on the right gives access into the ancient oak woods of the Cadair Idris National Nature Reserve. A constructed path climbs steeply up through the woods alongside the Nant Cadair, which plunges over a series of cascades. Here, in early summer, the wood may be heavy with the scent of rhododendron whose pink blossoms embellish the dark confines of this enchanting place, which must be one of the most picturesque starts to any mountain walk in Wales.

Once the broad leafed woodlands are left behind, the track climbs open grassy slopes into Cwm Cau, its dark waters only appearing at the last moment. Cwm Cau, a classic glacial cwm, is one of the great sights of Wales. It has the broken rocky face of Craig Cau as its centrepiece, with its buttresses and gullies producing a mosaic of dark grey rock and green patches of vegetation, an ideal habitat for alpine plants, some of which are here at their southernmost limit. To the left are the slopes of Craig Lwyd and to its right the bulky Penygadair.

A path now climbs steeply up the rocky crest of the ridge bounding the southern slopes of Cwm Cau. From the path, which clings to the edge of the cwm, you catch glimpses of the dark waters of Llyn Cau down narrow, plunging gullies, while to the south-west across Craig Cwm Amarch and the long rounded ridge of Mynydd Pencoed, the rich, green parallel valleys of Tal-y-llyn and Afon Dysynni look superb.

Continuing up the steep stony path you eventually cross the top of Craig Cau before descending along the cliff edge to level out at Bwlch Cau. Ahead, the path now climbs steeply up to the summit trig point and cairn of Penygadair (top of the seat) at 893m/2929 feet, just a small bump on the huge Cadair Idris ridge.

The low building near the summit is a refuge shelter, maintained by the National Park, and is a successor to a refreshment hut erected in the 1830s by the enterprising Dolgellau guide, Richard Pugh. Tourists used to flock here and after the long trek to the top were able to slake their thirst with a cup of hot tea. The more affluent visitors were able to engage a guide for the journey, which the diarist, the Rev. Francis Kilvert did in 1871. He obviously didn't enjoy the experience for he later wrote, 'Cadair Idris is the least interesting, dreariest, most desolate mountain I have ever known.' You obviously can't please everybody!

Maybe if their day had not been so wet and cloudy, Kilvert's impressions might have been different, for in clear weather the views from Idris's lofty perch are superb with most of the peaks in north and central Wales being visible. One special vista is the seaward one from the nearby lip of Cwm y Gadair – Idris's great northern cwm – across to the shimmering Mawddach Estuary and the pale strip of sand at Barmouth; beyond is the great sweep of Cardigan Bay, with the Lleyn Peninsula tapering into the Irish Sea. According to one legend, the Lleyn is the remains of a land bridge built by Idris across the sea to Ireland.

The impressive Cwm Cau, the highlight of the walk.

Penygadair seen from the Minffordd Path across Llyn Cau.

Above: *Scrambling up the Cyfrwy Arete.*

Below: *The Cyfrwy Arete seen from Penygadair.*

From the top of Penygadair you can easily contour round to the satellite rocky top of Cyfrwy (the saddle), a superb spot to admire the tremendous bird's-eye-view down into the cwm enclosing Llyn y Gadair. You can also look across to the impressive stratified north facing cliffs of Penygadair, and usually manage to pick out people gathered around the summit trig point. This huge natural amphitheatre is supposed to be where Idris reclined.

Cyfrwy is also famous for its superb jagged arete, one of the great scrambles of Wales, which is so well seen in profile from the summit of Penygadair. Sweeping up above scree slopes which plunge into the waters of Llyn y Gadair, this serrated Alpine-like ridge has a curious truncated quartz-topped tower known as The Table, discernible halfway up the route.

Scramblers take a rest on The Table on the Cyfrwy Arete.

Cwm Cau and Cadair Idris.

A bird's-eye-view of Llyn Cau from Craig Cau.

Penygadair to Minffordd

On a warm summer's evening the summit of Penygadair is a fine place to linger and watch the sun setting over the Mawddach Estuary before darkness forces you back to the creature comforts in the valleys. The most interesting way back to Minffordd is to head east from the rocky top of Penygadair and descend towards Mynydd Moel, passing the top of the infamous Fox's Path on the left whose steep, unstable scree slopes lead down to the shore of Llyn y Gadair. Sadly, due to increased erosion, this dangerous descent is presently discouraged by the National Park Authority. You also have improving views into Cwm Cau to the right.

From Mynydd Moel (bare mountain), a footpath plunges south–east down steep slopes to where you can cross the Nant Cadair stream – which can be difficult after heavy rain. Here the outward path near the ancient woodland exit gate is rejoined. If you are lucky the faint scent of rhododendron blossom will still hang in the evening air leaving a lasting memory of these very special hills as you stroll back down the zigzags to the car park.

INFORMATION

Start/Finish: The car park at Minffordd off the B4405 near the junction with the A487; GR: 732116.

Distance: 11km/7 miles.

Walking Time/total climb: About 6 hours/ 990m (3250 feet).

Grading: Very Difficult; a steep and strenuous ascent on mainly good paths. Care needed in wet and misty weather when traversing the lip of the huge cliffs of Cwm Cau.

Maps: OS Explorer OL 23.

Refreshments: Gwesty Minffordd Hotel near Tal-y-llyn Lake and numerous cafes and pubs in Dolgellau.

Transport: Buses from Aberystwyth to Porthmadog via Dolgellau stop here.

Heading up the edge of Cwm Cau, with Penygadair in the background.

THE TORRENT WALK

This short walk is a useful alternative when the weather on the tops is bad. To the east of Dolgellau, the Afon Clywedog plunges down a beautiful wooded gorge and over a series of cascades before it joins the Afon Wynion. This 2.5km/1½ mile easy walk along a good path overlooking a series of waterfalls is known as the Torrent Walk and it provides lovely views throughout. The walk, originally constructed by Thomas Payne, a surveyor and engineer, and his son, was laid out between 1799 and 1809. The walk is lovely at all times of the year but especially so in autumn, when rushing water tumbles over cascades and around moss-covered rocks overhung by tree branches cloaked in golden yellow and brown leaves.

The walk starts at a gate near the small lay-by on the B4416, Brithdir road, off the A470, about 4km/2½ miles from Dolgellau towards Machynlleth; GR 76118. From a small gate, signposted 'Torrent Walk', a footpath leads steeply down to a footbridge over the river. The footpath, with sections of steps, continues downstream through lovely deciduous woods on the left of the Afon Clywedog to a small gate on the minor road at Clywedog. You return by the same route, which offers a new perspective around each bend in the river.

Above and left: *The Afon Clywedog plunges down a rocky gorge on the Torrent Walk.*

The craggy Cyfrwy from Llyn y Gadair.

WALK 22   CADAIR IDRIS FROM THE DYSYNNI VALLEY

Most walkers ascending Cadair Idris use either the northern approach via the Pony Path from Ty Nant or the southern approach using the Minffordd path. However, this superb high-level walk approaches Cadair Idris from the head of the Dysynni Valley to the south-west. The circuit follows the southern section of the Pony Path to join the Ty Nant route up to Penygadair, finally returning over Craig Cwm Amarch and down the well-defined ridge of Mynydd Pencoed back into the Dysynni Valley. It is a varied walk through an ever-changing landscape rich in history and with some excellent views. For much of the walk you will see few other walkers.

This area to the south-west of Cadair Idris is a quiet and peaceful one with smooth sloping hills of grass and woodland overlooking the Dysynni Valley. It is a green and lush place with a flat floor through which the Afon Dysynni meanders from Cadair Idris to the sea near Tywyn.

The Pony Path – part of which is followed during the walk – was once the most direct way for locals to get to Dolgellau, their local market town. It starts from the hamlet of Llanfihangel-y-pennant which can be reached either by driving through the valley from the coast near Tywyn, or crossing a narrow hill road west from Abergynolwyn situated just south-west of Tal-y-llyn Lake.

Although this outing may not be the most dramatic approach to Cadair Idris, it does allow you to discover a beautiful corner of Wales, and you can explore the ancient ruins of Castell y Bere sited on a rocky outcrop near the start of the walk. An ascent of the craggy peak of Craig yr Aderyn (Bird Rock) thrusting up from green fields further down the valley, and famous as an inland breeding site for cormorants, is highly recommended.

Llanfihangel–y–pennant to Penygadair

From a small car park at Llanfihangel-y-pennant, a narrow lane leads up the valley passing Tyn y Fach farmhouse to a bridge over the Afon Cadair. The ruined cottage of Tyn-y-ddol to the right has a commemorative stone to the memory of Mary Jones who lived there. In 1800, aged only sixteen, she walked barefoot for 42km/25 miles over the mountains to Bala to buy a Welsh bible from the Reverend Thomas Charles, a Methodist minister there. It is said that Mary's devotion impressed him so much that he began a campaign from which grew the British and Foreign Bible Society.

The surfaced track continues past the old farmhouse of Gwastadfryn then climbs steadily through a larch wood, before a waymarked path branches right to cross a feeder stream. The path climbs up through a rocky area sparsely wooded with oak trees eventually rejoining the track once more just beyond a conspicuous standing stone. From here you have an excellent view back to Castell y Bere, with the rounded hump of Mynydd Pencoed on your right and Penygadair thrusting its top above the skyline ahead.

After contouring round the hill, the Pony Path veers up left into a side-valley to the remote sheep pens in the old farmyard of Hafotty Gwastadfryn. Beyond here a track crosses a stream at a ford and zigzags steeply to the right up grassy slopes, finally heading to the conspicuous col on the skyline ahead. You eventually arrive at a junction of fences and join the constructed track with its stone flags and steps to control erosion on the popular northern section of the Pony Path climbing up from Ty Nant. Here the views open out and you get a grand view north over the Mawddach Estuary to the Rhinogau.

The view from Cyfrwy to Penygadair.

Looking from Penygadair to Cyfrwy backed by the Mawddach Estuary.

The last stage of the ascent is now east from the col up a broad path which soon climbs steeply up a series of zigzags until you top the rise and are rewarded by a view of Penygadair. Up till now the path has avoided the great cliffs above Llyn y Gadair, but a slight detour left at a junction along an obvious wide stony track, takes you up to the satellite rocky top of Cyfrwy (the saddle) for a better view. From this superb vantage point you can admire the tremendous bird's-eye-view down into the cwm enclosing Llyn y Gadair and also get a detailed perspective of the impressive three-tiered, stratified north face of Penygadair.

Penygadair (top of the seat) now beckons along the path around the edge of the rocky cwm, requiring considerable care in misty weather or in snow and ice conditions when cornices often form here. The stony path soon lands you at the trig point and summit cairn at 893m/2929 feet. If you've picked a good day (close proximity to the sea often pushes cloud and rain across the rocky summit), you will be rewarded by tremendous panoramic views ranging from Pumlumon in the south to the Snowdon range in the north.

Penygadair to Llanfihangel-y-pennant

Descending south-east from the summit of Penygadair, the upper section of the Minffordd Path is followed which overlooks the impressive Cwm Cau with Llyn Cau sheltered in a hollow below its spectacular cliffs. A steep climb beyond a col takes you up to the summit of Craig Cwm Amarch (Amarch valley rock) overlooking Tal-y-llyn Lake to the south.

The way is now south-west along the crest of the clearly defined ridge to Mynydd Pencoed. At the end of the ridge, steep slopes with springy turf underfoot, now drop steeply west to the small farm buildings at Pencoed. From here a footpath passes through fields to the south to join a track, which can be followed to the lane for Llanfihangel-y-pennant.

Opposite page: *Evening light illuminates Cadair Idris at the head of the Dysynni Valley.*

The great wall of Cadair Idris seen from the north-west.

INFORMATION

Start/Finish: Small car park at Llanfihangel-y-pennant, GR: 672089.

Distance: 16.5km/10 miles.

Walking Time/total climb: 6 hours/1060m (3500 feet).

Grading: Difficult; a steep ascent on mainly good paths. Care needed in wet and misty weather when traversing above the huge cliffs of Cwm Cau.

Maps: OS Explorer OL23.

Refreshments: Gwesty Minffordd Hotel near Tal-y-llyn Lake or various pubs and cafes in Tywyn.

Transport: No public transport.

Above: *Penygadair, the highest point on the Cadair Idris range.*

Right: *The ruins of Castell y Bere, situated on a rocky mound, in its secluded location at the head of the Dysynni Valley with the Cadair Idris range rising behind it.*

Castell y Bere

The isolated ruins of Castell y Bere are situated on a rocky outcrop (GR: 667085) overlooking broad, green fields and the nearby Afon Dysynni. Although the ruins do not rise to any great height, the restored remains give a fascinating glimpse into the past and are worth exploring. The elongated shape of the crag dictated the layout of the castle and its defences were enhanced by the use of rock-cut ditches. A small lay-by below the outcrop gives access to the ruins.

The castle has a fascinating history. It was built by Llewelyn the Great in the early 1220's and guarded what was once an important route through the mountains. In 1283 the castle was besieged by over 3,000 men, and eventually fell to the forces of Edward I. The castle was then repaired and strengthened by the English over the next ten years until it was attacked in 1294 during a Welsh uprising led by Madog ap Llewelyn. Badly damaged, the castle was eventually abandoned and consigned to seven centuries of obscurity and decay.

The flat-bottomed Dysynni Valley seen from Craig yr Aderyn (Bird Rock).

Craig yr Aderyn (Bird Rock)

The crag of Craig yr Aderyn, an important SSSI, rises to over 250m/820 feet above the surrounding green fields on the south side of the Dysynni Valley, and is a traditional breeding and roosting site for chough and a rare inland nesting site of cormorants. Despite the fact that the sea has receded about 8km/5 miles over the centuries, the cormorants have remained loyal to the spot and pairs still return to breed. In fact the lower reaches of the valley just north of Tywyn are still named 'Broadwater' on the OS map.

From a small lay-by (GR: 651076) at the foot of Craig yr Aderyn, an excellent out-and-back walk of about 2.5km/1½ miles can be enjoyed to its rocky top. A signed track leads south from the lay-by to a gate. Here, a grassy path strikes off right up the hillside, passing some steep crags, before taking a meandering line up a broad ridge to the airy summit of Bird Rock. From here you have excellent views of the Dysynni Valley, especially north-west to Castell y Bere backed by the endless grassy slopes of Mynydd Pencoed and the brooding summit of Penygadair.

The shapely Craig yr Aderyn (Bird Rock).

The craggy profile of Tyrrau Mawr.

This circular walk explores the quieter and less dramatic hills on the western flanks of the Cadair Idris range as it descends gently towards the sea. It is mainly easy walking along a craggy escarpment, with splendid views of Barmouth and the Mawddach Estuary. The walk also passes through an area rich in history with several standing stones and other ancient sites.

An excellent starting point is the large car park at Llynnau (lakes) Cregennen. These two charming lakes are approached up a narrow hill road from just north of Arthog village on the Dolgellau road, which runs along the southern shore of the Afon Mawddach. The steep road climbs up through a landscape of green meadows, wooded foothills and rocky knolls covered in heather before the two lakes suddenly come into view backed by the craggy escarpment of Tyrrau Mawr on the main Cadair Idris ridge. On the left shore is a boathouse overlooked by the small pointed peak of Bryn Brith. Owned by the National Trust, the lakes are a popular beauty spot and picnic area.

Lynnau Cregennen to Braich Ddu

From the car park the narrow lane continues south-east, skirting the larger lake, to a T-junction. Just before the junction you pass a conspicuous standing stone on your left, one of several to be found on the western flanks of Cadair Idris and thought to have been originally used as markers for early travellers through this area.

The right fork of the hill road leads past the ruined buildings of Haffoty-fach farm, and after about 0.5km/⅓ mile an ancient track known as the Black Road (or

Ffordd Ddu) is followed left as it slants up across the northern flanks of Braich Ddu. A short distance up the track, a grassy hillock topped by another impressive solitary standing stone comes into view on your right. A short detour allows a closer look.

Eventually the track climbs up to a gate at the edge of a forestry plantation. Hidden among the trees a short distance to the south-west is the round, burial cairn of Bedd y Brenin meaning 'grave of the king'. It is about 30m/98 feet in diameter and was first excavated in 1851 when the obvious damage was caused. A capstone was found covering a burial cist and now forms part of a wall built over the cairn at some later date.

Our way is now left alongside a wire fence up a broad grassy east ridge on Braich Ddu, as it climbs above the grey cliffs of Craig Cwm-llwyd. From the escarpment you have splendid views north-west to the conspicuous railway bridge spanning the mouth of the Mawddach Estuary to Barmouth, whose shimmering sands are overlooked by gentle hills at the southern end of the Rhinogau. A final short climb leads up to a broad grassy moor from where you can look north-east across a grassy cwm whose rim sweeps round to the sharp profile of the rocky cliffs of Craig-las, on Tyrrau Mawr's north-western face.

Braich Ddu to Lynnau Cregennen

Continuing south on a faint path alongside the wire fence, a gentle descent leads to a grassy dip, from where you can look down left to the lovely isolated Llyn Cyri in a hollow below the dark cliffs of Craig-y-llyn. A short climb beyond the grassy dip takes you up to the edge of the shattered rocky escarpment of Craig-y-llyn. Grassy slopes finally lead up to the subsidiary top, with its ancient mound of stones – shown on the OS map as Twll yr Ogof – then on to the main top. From beside a small slate cairn at the summit you can really appreciate the seaward views stretching to the Lleyn and Bardsey Island. To the south you can easily pick out Craig yr Aderyn, backed by the flatlands of Dyffryn Dysynni while east, the skyline is dominated by Cyfrwy and Penygadair.

A standing stone backed by Tyrrau Mawr.

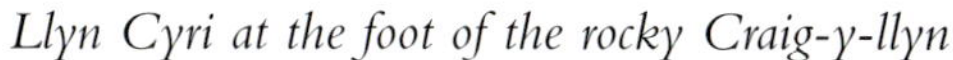

Llyn Cyri at the foot of the rocky Craig-y-llyn.

INFORMATION
Start/Finish: National Trust car park at Llynnau Cregennen, GR: 658143.
Distance: 14km/8¾ miles.
Walking Time/total climb: About 5 hours/420m (1378 feet).
Grading: Moderate; a high-level walk mainly on good paths and tracks.
Maps: OS Explorer OL23.
Refreshments: Various pubs and cafes in Dolgellau.
Transport: No public transport to the start but a bus service between Dolgellau and Tywyn stops at Arthog.

Another gentle descent north-east soon leads to a dip overlooking the conspicuous scar of a farm track climbing up right from Hafotty Gwastadfryn. Beyond the dip, a steady climb up grassy slopes lands you at the summit of Tyrrau Mawr, at 661m/2169 feet, the highest point of the walk and, not surprisingly, offering tremendous views.

On its northern slopes the steep grass-topped cliffs of Craig-las sweep down to a minor road leading back to Llynnau Creggenen. From the summit of Tyrrau Mawr a footpath leads past the conspicuous stony outcrop of Carnedd Lwyd to join the Pony Path at the lowest point on the escarpment at Rhiw Gwredydd.

The constructed zigzags of the popular Pony Path, with its anti-erosion stone steps, descends north-east down towards Ty Nant, and, after about 800m/875 yards, a path branching off to the left takes you down to the narrow hill road leading left back to the Cregennen Lakes. Heading south-west along the tarmaced road for about 1.2km/¾ mile, you reach a cattle grid from where a farm track veers off right. Along the track a waymarked footpath bypasses the farm and you soon reach the northern shore of the larger of the two Cregennen Lakes. A faint grassy path through heather around the lake edge soon leads back to the car park and the end of the walk.

However, if time permits, then an ascent of the pointed peak of Bryn Brith, which overlooks the lake, is a must. A path ascends the steep heather-clad south-west ridge and twists its way through numerous hollows and around outcrops up to the summit at 383m/1257 feet, from where you have a magnificent outlook to the coast, the Rhinogau and towards Cadair Idris itself.

Heather and the golden flowers of gorse create a colourful foreground of this view above Llyn Cregennen, with the Cadair Idris range in the background.

Above: *The small shapely peak of Bryn Brith over-looking Llynnau Creggenen.*

Left: *Cadair Idris seen across the Mawddach Estuary from near Barmouth.*

Below: *Sunrise across Llynnau Creggenen.*

9 THE LLEYN PENINSULA

Yr Eifl at sunset.

*Yr Eifl seen from the west across
the beach at Porth Dinllaen.*

To the south of Angelsey lies the long, low Lleyn Peninsula (the Lleyn or Llyn), a largely unspoilt area warmed by the Gulf Stream and forming the great curve of Caernarfon Bay. Much of its coastline, including Bardsey Island at the very western tip, has now been designated as Heritage Coast. Most of the heritage coast is also included in the Lleyn Area of Outstanding Natural Beauty (AONB).

Although outside the Snowdonia National Park, the Lleyn has a varied landscape ranging from steep, jagged cliffs near Aberdaron to wide sandy bays with sand dunes, bathing beaches (notably Porth Neigwl) and little fishing villages. Inland there is a rolling green landscape with small villages and white-washed farms surrounded by small, hedgerowed fields. The Lleyn has been populated since early times and here you will find Iron Age hill forts, remarkable Megalithic chambered tombs dating back to 2000BC, ancient trackways, cairns and standing stones.

The island of Bardsey (or Enlli) about 2km/1¼ miles off the tip of Llyen, also played a role in the rich history of the peninsula. Christianity was brought to the island by Augustinian canons in the thirteenth century, and they built the extensive abbey of St.Mary of Bardsey, of which part of the thirteenth century tower still remains. In the Middle Ages the Abbey was a popular destination for thousands of pilgrims. Many chose to end their days there, hence the tradition that 20,000 'saints' are buried on the island. Three pilgrimages to Bardsey was thought to be equivalent to one to Rome.

Today there are still pilgrimages to Bardsey, which is now a National Nature Reserve owned and run by Bardsey Island Trust, and is famous for its seabird sanctuary and large population of grey seals. The finest view of Bardsey is from the wild headland of Uwchmynydd, which is easily approached along a 3.2km/2 miles National Trust path from Aberdaron; once the port for pilgrims on their way to Bardsey.

Much of the Lleyn coastline can be explored along a series of good footpaths and, from a hill walker's point of view, there are a few excellent little peaks to explore. The best of these is that bold upthrust of the triple-topped Yr Eifl (the fork), also known as The Rivals. Yr Eifl is such a conspicuous feature of the northern Lleyn when seen from Angelsey's western seaboard or from the high north-western peaks of Snowdonia. Seen at dusk across Cardigan Bay from any of the golden beaches near Harlech, the impressive silhouette of the shapely Yr Eifl sends out an invitation to walkers seeking new areas to explore. And a bonus is that Yr Eifl is also often free of cloud when the higher tops of Snowdonia are still cloaked in mist.

Looking north-east from Tre'r Ceiri to Gyrn Ddu and along the coastline.

Approaching Tre'r Ceiri.

The western prong of Yr Eifl.

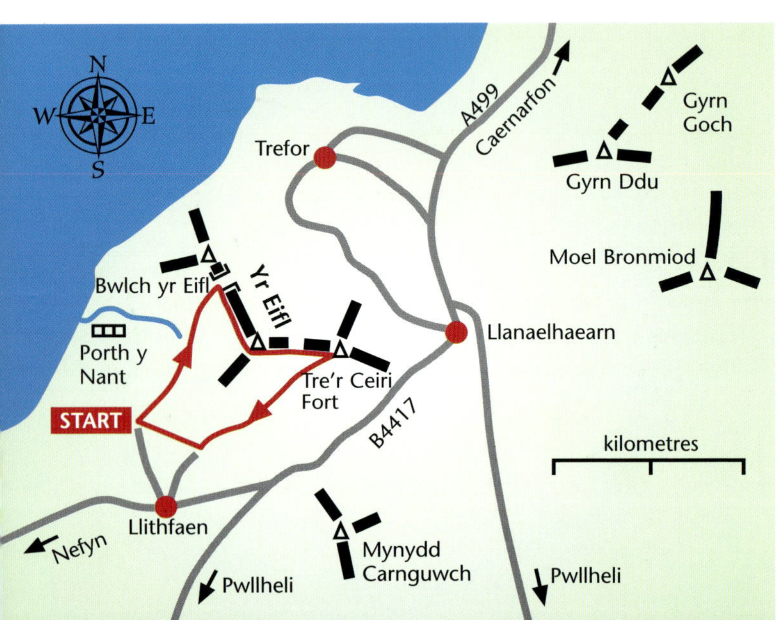

WALK 24   YR EIFL (THE RIVALS)

Although only rising to just 564m/1850 feet above sea level, and despite some scars left by quarrying activities, Yr Eifl (also known as The Rivals) provides a splendid walk offering great viewpoints on clear days. The outing is also full of historical interest, especially the partly-restored Iron Age hill fort of Tre'r Ceiri on the eastern summit of Yr Eifl. Moreover, Yr Eifl can often give a sunlit day when the Snowdonia hills are sulking under a cloud canopy.

The trio of tops that make up Yr Eifl lie on the north side of the Lleyn Peninsula overlooking the village of Trefor, and are situated 19km/12miles down the Pwllheli road from Caernarfon.

Llithfaen to Tre'r Ceiri

The walk starts at a car park on a narrow lane just north of the village of Llithfaen on the B4417 Trefor to Nefyn road. A bridleway climbs north up through heather-covered slopes to the pass of Bwlch yr Eifl, which separates the northern and central peaks. A hidden valley down to the left is known as Nant Gwrtheyrn, said to be named after the fifth century leader Vortigern. At the foot of the valley is the Victorian village of Porth y Nant, a quarry village which was established about 1863. After the demand for granite faltered in the late 1950s, the place was abandoned and allowed to fall into ruin. Since 1978 the village has been restored and is now the Welsh National Language Centre.

Just beyond the top of the pass opposite a gated track giving access to a conspicuous communications mast and old granite quarry, a path leads to the right. This climbs up broad, easy-angled heather slopes and scree to the top of the highest of the Rival hills, the central prong of the fork –Yr Eifl – at 564m/1850 feet, its summit marked by a large cairn and trig point.

142

This is a magnificent viewpoint, arguably one of the best in North Wales. You can gaze along the Lleyn Peninsula and on a clear day the peaks of Snowdonia fill the eastern horizon, while across the waters of Cardigan Bay the mountains of the Harlech Dome are visible. While further south is Mynydd Presli, source of the bluestones used to build Stonehenge. To the north is Anglesey and maybe on a very clear day you can pick out the distant Wicklow Mountains, across the Irish Sea to the west.

Leaving the summit in an easterly direction towards the next top (Tre'r Ceiri), a faint path weaves its way down through boulders and heather to a broad col. It's best not to leave the path otherwise you end up struggling through boulders hidden beneath heather – a bit like the Rhinogau. Beyond the broad dip the path continues up heather slopes to an obvious gap in the outer defensive wall of the ancient settlement.

Continuing up the path you pass through the inner wall of the extensive Iron Age hill fort of Tre'r Ceiri, which crowns the summit of the eastern peak of Yr Eifl. Once through the gap the actual summit at 485m (1591feet) is reached by going left alongside the wall.

Tre'r Ceiri is one of the most remarkable fortified village hill forts in Wales. Significant drystone ramparts surround its entire circuit, with clearly visible entrances and staggered gateways. In places some of the stones, up to 5m/15 feet in height, are still standing. These are some of the best preserved remains of an Iron Age hill fort in the whole of Britain. The site occupies about 2.5ha/6.2 acres and its interior is packed with walled stone buildings and the remains of about 150 huts with some walls still standing. Some are round houses, while others are rectangular or oval.

Much restoration work has been carried out and archaeologists estimate that the site could have supported a population of up to 400, and may have been continuously occupied for many hundreds of years. It is thought that the earliest parts date from the centuries before the Roman invasion of Wales in AD78. It was certainly occupied during the latter part of the Roman occupation when additional defences and huts were added: all of the excavated finds are dated 150-400 A.D. The fort appears to have been abandoned in the fourth century AD.

The summit of Tre'r Ceiri.

One of many remains of walled huts in the Tre'r Ceiri Fort.

INFORMATION

Start/Finish: Car park about 1km to the north of Llithfaen GR:353441.

Distance: 8km/5 miles.

Walking Time/total climb: 4 hours/425m (1400 feet).

Grading: Moderate; a strenuous walk, mainly on good paths and with great views throughout.

Maps: OS Explorer 254, Lleyn Peninsula East.

Refreshments: Pubs at Trefor and Llanaelhaearn.

Transport: Llithfaen is on a bus route from Trefor to Tudweilog; also buses from Pwllheli.

The central prong of Yr Eifl seen from Tre'r Ceiri.

The summit is yet another great vantage point for views of the Lleyn and the seas around it, and especially north-east across the A499 to the shapely peaks of Gyrn Ddu and Bwlch Mawr with the serrated coastline to their left.

Tre'r Ceiri to Llithfaen

A path leads south-west from the summit of Tre'r Ceiri back through the boundary walls to join a well-maintained path. The path descends through heather to a broad dip before veering right to a drystone wall, which is crossed by a ladder stile.

Ahead the path climbs steadily across moorland to the right of the rocky outcrop of Caergribin. Beyond the rise the path descends south-west into a broad valley where a wide grassy track is joined leading towards a white house. About 180m/200 yards before the house is reached, a good track alongside a wall climbs north-west over heather moorland back to the road and car park.

144